"Hear what posterity will say of us. It will say that this was a generation of giants, because it carried out a task which had been impossible for many generations and many centuries." Thus the Neapolitan patriot Luigi Settembrini described the men who, little more than a century ago, fought to free Italy from tyranny and foreign rule and created a new independent nation.

In 1815 unification seemed impossible. There were two independent states – Naples, ruled by a French king, and Piedmont. Central Italy, and the historic capital, Rome, were under the Pope's rule. Lombardy and Venice formed part of the vast conglomerate Austrian Empire, and Modena, Parma, Tuscany and Lucca had puppets of the Austrians for rulers. Poverty and oppression were almost universal, and opponents of arbitrary government were viciously repressed.

The author tells how new ideas of nationalism and liberalism slowly took hold. He uses memoirs, letters and diplomatic papers to record the first stirrings of rebellion and the self-sacrifice of idealists such as Mazzini. The heroic story of Garibaldi's campaign in the south is told in graphic detail; but the quieter achievements of the statesman Cavour are shown to have been equally important. From 1848, when people throughout Europe rose against tyranny, to 1870, when Victor Emmanuel of Piedmont entered Rome as first King of Italy, we learn the story through the words of its heroes, as well as the many fascinated observers from other countries.

The people and the background to this epic adventure are brought to life in about fifty drawings, prints, maps and photographs.

The Unification of Italy

CHRISTOPHER LEEDS

WAYLAND PUBLISHERS · LONDON

G. P. PUTNAM'S SONS · NEW YORK

NOTE ON PLACE-NAMES

PIEDMONT, SARDINIA, SAVOY – The Kingdom of Sardinia included
the mainland districts of Piedmont, Savoy, Genoa and Nice as
well as the island of Sardinia. It was ruled by kings of the House
of Savoy. Since Piedmont was the most populous area, and the
capital, Turin, was situated there, the whole country was usually
known as Piedmont.
SICILY, NAPLES, THE TWO SICILIES – The Kingdom of the Two
Sicilies included the island of Sicily and the Italian mainland south
of the Papal States. The capital was Naples, and the country was
often called the Kingdom of Naples.

Frontispiece King Victor Emmanuel drives through the Corso in Rome as
Italians celebrate the final unification of their country

SBN (England): 85340 384 8
SBN (United States): 399-11323-1
Library of Congress Catalogue Card Number: 73-93349

Set in 'Monophoto' Times and printed offset litho in Great Britain by
Page Bros (Norwich) Ltd, Norwich

Contents

The Illustrations

Map

1 The Idea of Unity

"HEAR WHAT POSTERITY will say of us. It will say that this was a generation of giants, because it carried out a task which had been impossible for many generations and many centuries. This generation made Italy . . ."[1] Thus spoke the Neapolitan teacher and literary critic Luigi Settembrini in 1879, when Italy had been a united nation for nine years.

Since the collapse of the Roman Empire in the fifth century A.D., and the invasion of Europe by the Goths and Huns from the East, the Italian peninsula had been divided into many small independent states. Keen rivalry, both political and commercial, had intensified their division. Foreign help had always been welcome in the repeated local wars, and European powers such as Spain, France and the Austrian Empire had been invited by the Italians themselves to compete for influence in the area.

Divided country

During the later Middle Ages, Venice and Genoa, in the north-east and north-west of the country, had been rich and powerful states, controlling the shipping in the Mediterranean Sea and in particular the profitable spice trade with the Far East. This prosperity came to an end with the discovery of the sea route round southern African, the wars between France and Spain in Italy in the sixteenth century, and the rise of England and Holland as great trading nations.

By the eighteenth century no Italian state could claim any importance in European affairs. Lombardy was part of the Austrian (Hapsburg) Empire, ruled from Vienna, which included territory in Germany, Hungary, Bohemia, Slovakia, the Balkans and the Netherlands. An Austrian also ruled the Grand Duchy

Austrian Empire

Opposite Pope Pius IX proceeding to mass at St. Peter's Cathedral on Christmas Eve 1847

of Tuscany, which had formerly been the independent city-states of Florence, Siena and Pisa. The Kingdom of the Two Sicilies (Naples and Sicily) had as their monarchs a junior branch of the Spanish Bourbons. In central Italy, the Papal States, ruled by the Pope, seemed an impassable obstacle to the hope of union between north and south. An even greater obstacle was the slowness of most Italians to understand the idea of unity – few of them knew or cared what happened outside their own little part of the peninsula.

Sardinia   In 1720 Savoy, a small French-speaking state in the Alps, gained the Italian island of Sardinia, and its Duke was allowed to take the title of King. This event was later seen to have been of crucial importance, for it was the activities of this ambitious dynasty which did much to create the united Italian nation.

The *Risorgimento* – an Italian word which suggests the idea of awakening and the recovery of strength – was perhaps the most important event in Italian history. It was an exciting and romantic period for those who lived through it and fought to create the country that they wanted; it was also remarkable, because until the 1840s few people imagined that the barriers in the way of unity would ever be overcome.

The word *Risorgimento* sums up three distinct aims: the expulsion of foreign rulers from Italy; the overthrow of harsh and tyrannical governments and the creation of free political institutions; and the unification of the fragmented country into a free independent state. During the eighteenth century reformers,
The   philosophers and patriots, with some or all of these ideas in
Enlightenment   mind, tried to awaken a new spirit in Italy. In the rest of Europe writers such as Jean-Jacques Rousseau had put forward the idea that men should be able to live under whatever form of government they wanted; monarchs such as Joseph II of Austria had taken notice of these theories and had given their people a greater measure of freedom. In Italy, too, the patriots were encouraged when they saw some local rulers carry out a few enlightened reforms. Still, however, the average Italian was a poor peasant, illiterate, living on the edge of starvation, and with no say in the way he was governed.

10   Italy had a great cultural tradition, starting with classical and

Christian Rome. During the later Middle Ages and the Renaissance, it had been the artistic and intellectual centre of Europe. The achievements of writers such as Dante and Boccaccio, artists such as Raphael, Leonardo da Vinci and Michaelangelo, Machiavelli the political thinker and Galileo the scientist, formed a tradition which could not easily be ignored. Nor had the achievements of free elected governments in Genoa, Venice and Florence been forgotten. To a few prominent Italians it seemed humiliating that in the eyes of the world the magnificence of their past was contrasted with their present poverty and decay. Antonio Genovese, professor of political economy at Naples, saw the divisions between the states as the chief barrier to economic progress. Pietro Giannone, a Neapolitan historian, pointed out that the great influence of the Catholic church made political change very difficult. Such men, however, were always in a minority, without great influence on the mass of Italians.

The occupation of the country by Napoleon Bonaparte (1769–1821), Emperor of the French, gave great help to the cause of unity. In 1796 Napoleon invaded northern Italy, presenting himself as a liberator rather than a conqueror. He was, after all, of Italian blood – his birthplace, Corsica, had only been sold by Genoa to France in 1768. In any case it was good government rather than national government that most politically conscious citizens desired, and this the Napoleonic code of law and system of administration supplied. *Napoleon Bonaparte*

All the existing kings were deposed, except in the islands of Sardinia and Sicily which, protected by the British Navy, retained their independence under the Kings of Piedmont and Naples. Napoleon's plan was to remove the power of the great landowners and also of the priests. The Pope was evicted from Rome, and the temporal power of the Church taken over until 1814. Thus Napoleon destroyed the idea that the rulers were immovable, challenged the authority of the Papacy, and reduced the number of states to three – Piedmont, Naples and his own conquered territory, which he termed the Cisalpine Republic. French revolutionary ideas, summed up by the slogan "Liberty, Equality, Fraternity," suggested what might be achieved by a united people; what had been a cultural and literary tradition,

11

kept alive by a few writers and thinkers, now came to mean something to the mass of Italians.

Congress of Vienna With the fall of Napoleon in 1815, however, the Congress of Vienna divided Italy, handing back the states to their former rulers. The Bourbons were restored to the Kingdom of the Two Sicilies (Naples and Sicily), and the Pope regained his temporal power in the Central States. In the north the House of Savoy recovered Piedmont and Sardinia, whose territories were extended to include Savoy, Nice and the former Republic of Genoa.

Prince Metternich, the Austrian Chancellor, who presided at the Congress, was determined that Italy should be kept divided and weak, so Austria was given Venetia, in addition to Lombardy, her former possession, and thus became dominant in northern Italy. In Tuscany the Austrian Emperor's brother, Grand Duke Ferdinand III, was restored. Parma was given to the Emperor's daughter Marie-Louise, the former wife of Napoleon I, and Modena to his cousin Francis IV. The tiny states of Lucca and Massa-Carrara were earmarked for future annexation by Tuscany. Military rights were secured in all these countries, and *The Quadrilateral* Metternich had an army of 70,000 men within the Quadrilateral, a group of four strong fortresses bounded by rivers, situated in a powerful central position in Lombardy. He also made a military alliance with Naples. From then on he was constantly able to assert Austria's right to interfere in Italy.

Subservice to a foreign power was not the only obstacle to unity. Regional and municipal differences were enormous. Giuseppe Mazzini, leading agitator for the freedom and unity of Italy, declared: "We have no flag, no political name, no rank among European nations. We have no common centre, no common fact, no common market. We are dismembered into eight states – Lombardy, Parma, Tuscany, Modena, Lucca, the Popedom, Piedmont, the Kingdom of Naples – all independent of one another, without alliance, without unity of aim, without organized connection between them . . . Eight different systems of currency, weights and measures, civil, commercial and penal legislation, of administrative organization and of police restriction, divide us and render us as much as possible strangers to each other."[2]

12

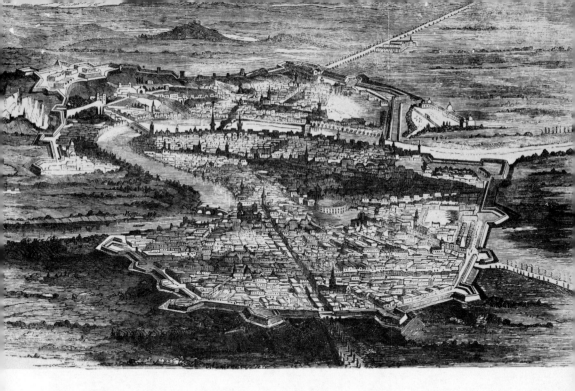

The Austrian military presence in Italy – the fortifications of Verona, one of the towns of the Quadrilateral

The ducato coinage of Naples differed from the oncia of Sicily, the Papal scudo and the Piedmontese lira. Twenty-two different customs barriers existed along the Po river, an example of the municipal separatism, or *campanilismo*, which impeded unity and progress in industry and agriculture. The Neapolitan historian Luigi Blanch said in 1851: "The patriotism of the Italians is like that of the ancient Greeks and is love of a single town, not of a country; it is the feeling of a tribe, not of a nation. Only by a foreign conquest have they ever been united. Leave them to themselves and they split into fragments."[3]

"The feeling of a tribe"

The Florentine disliked the Venetian, who in turn looked down on the Neapolitan, while the Sicilian was resentful of any suggestion that he might come from the mainland. An article by Gianrinaldo Carli, published in 1764–6, shows the common attitude towards newcomers: "He looked at the stranger with a superior smile, then asked him if he was a foreigner. The latter

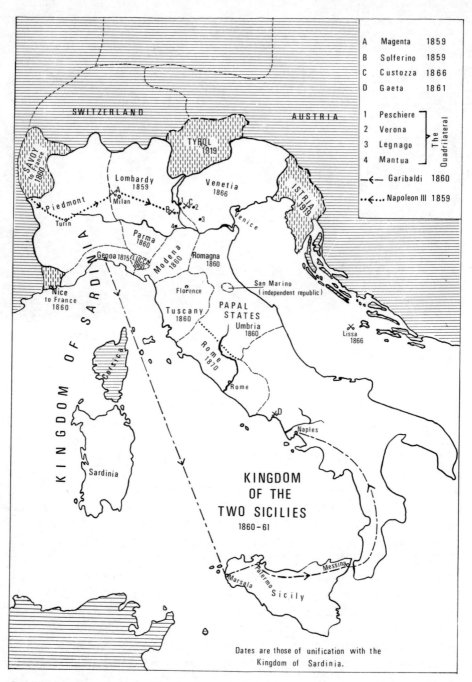

Italy during the period of unification. The area shown in white was the Kingdom of Italy
from 1870 to 1919.

glanced at his questioner from top to toe, and with a composed and nonchalant air replied, 'No, Sir.' 'You are Milanese then?' rejoined the other. 'No, Sir, I am not Milanese.' At this reply the questioner showed great surprise . . . and after the most sincere protestation of not understanding, sought an explanation. 'I am Italian,' replied the stranger, 'and an Italian is never a foreigner, just as a Frenchman is not a foreigner in France, an Englishman in England, a Dutchman in Holland and so on'."[4] In general there was a lack of acceptance or even understanding of the idea of Italy. Was unity possible or really desirable? Who could bring the states together to chase out the Austrian overlord? *Is it possible?* Many felt perhaps it was better to allow foreigners to carry out the unpleasant task of government, which left them open to blame when things went wrong.

The Italians had retained some sense of a common heritage from the Renaissance of the fifteenth century and beyond. They all spoke the same language, even though the natural speech of most Italians was dialect, which might not be understood outside its own particular district; they shared the same Catholic religion – the Pope and most Cardinals were usually Italian; though rarely acting in common, they shared a historical heritage stretching back to the Roman Empire; and Rome itself stood as a monument reminding them of their former greatness. These patriotic sentiments were repeatedly appealed to by poets and writers. Giacomo Leopardi (1798–1837) sought to inspire Italians to action:

> "I see the walls and arches, O my Italy,
> The columns and the images, the lone
> Towers of our ancestors,
> But this I do not see,
> The glorious laurel and the swords they bore
> In ancient times . . .
> Who brought her to this state? – and this is worse,
> That both her arms are bound about with chains . . .
> Weep, for you have good cause, my Italy"[5]

Discontent under absolute government was fostered by the secret societies, the most famous being the "Carbonari" or

"Charcoal-burners," which existed in Naples and Sicily from 1806 and slowly spread its influence through every state in Italy. Its principles were derived partly from the anti-clerical French freemasons, partly from obscure Italian traditions. Its motto was "Despotism Annihilated," depicted on a medal as the Goddess of Liberty slaying the Dragon of Tyranny. Members pledged themselves to revolt, with signatures written in blood.

The Carbonari The aims and memberships of the clubs, however, varied so much from state to state that their power was purely regional and they had no country-wide plan. For example the vague aims of the "Society of Guelph Knights" were: "The independence of Italy, our Country. To give her a single, constitutional government, or at least to unite the various Italian governments in a confederation; all governments, however, shall be based on a constitution, freedom of the press and of worship, the same laws, currency and measures."[6]

The societies' members were mostly articulate middle-class people – small property owners, town officials, lawyers and army officers – who had perhaps suffered some injustice under the existing system. They campaigned against the grievance they themselves had felt, perhaps civil service inefficiency, priestly rule or uncontrolled brigandage. However, beyond blaming everything on the Austrians, it was hard to agree on a common solution to all these problems.

Byron Foreigners who saw Imperial Rome and Renaissance Florence as the birthplaces of their own culture were interested in developments in Italy. The English poet and romantic, Lord Byron, who was to die in 1824 helping the Greek revolt against Turkey, supported the Carbonari. He kept a journal at Ravenna in January and February 1821 in which he recorded: "Today I have had no communication with my Carbonari cronies; but in the mean time my lower apartments are full of their bayonets, fusils, cartridges and what not. I suppose that they consider me as a depot, to be sacrificed in case of accidents! It is no great matter, supposing that Italy could be liberated, who or what is sacrificed. It is a grand object – the very *poetry* of politics. Only think! A free Italy! Why, there has been nothing like it since the days of Augustus."[7]

The Caffè Greco in Rome, where artists and revolutionaries met and talked

The Carbonari continually plotted against the governments. Any conspirators arrested could expect imprisonment or even death. In Venice, in December 1821, "More than thirty of the Carbonari of Polesine were led out between lines of white-coated solidiers on to a scaffold erected in front of the Ducal Palace, from the balcony of which their sentence was pronounced. The Imperial clemency commuted the death penalty for long years of imprisonment in chains in various fortresses beyond the Alps – the leaders being consigned to the noisome cells of the Spielberg fortress in Moravia whence several of them never emerged alive."[8]

Silvio Pellico, one of the Carbonari arrested in October 1820 for a fairly trivial offence, suffered ten years in prison in the Spielberg in Bohemia. He wrote a famous book, *Le Mie Prigioni* (My Prisons), first published in 1832, which was said to have damaged Austria more than a lost battle. Metternich tried in vain to get the Pope to put it on the Index of Prohibited Books in the Papal States. Pellico describes the occasion when he and his companions were told that they had been set free at last. The Chief of Police said:

"'Gentlemen . . . I have the pleasure . . . the honour . . . to inform you . . . that His Majesty the Emperor has granted you . . . yet another favour . . .'

He hestitated to tell us what this favour might be. We thought it must be some slight mitigation in our sentence, such as exemption from the nuisance of work, or an extra book or two, or maybe even less revolting food.

'But,' he said, 'do you not understand?'

'No Sir, please be good enough to tell us what this favour is.'

'It's freedom for both of you, and a third, who will soon be in your arms.'"[9]

I. G. Capaldi, the translator of this book, described how the work the prisoners had to do "consisted of sawing wood, preparing lint for dressing wounds, and making stockings from wool so impregnated with oil and grease that the stench of it brought on splitting headaches. The prisoners had to hand in a pair of these stockings every week under penalty of severe punishment. As these stockings had to be made . . . in the perpetual gloom of the dungeons it is not surprising that the prisoners preferred to be punished for not handing in their weekly quota rather than submit to the torture of working in such conditions."[10]

Reactionary societies
In the Papal States the Carbonari faced bitter opposition from a group of religious crusaders known as the Sanfedesti, a counter-revolutionary secret society supported by nobles, townspeople and peasants alike. Its oath of allegiance was: "I swear to remain steadfast in the defence of the holy cause which I have embraced, not to spare anyone belonging to the notorious gang of liberals, regardless of his birth, lineage or fortune; to show no pity for the wailing of children or the old; and to spill the blood of the infamous liberals to the last drop, regardless of sex or rank. Finally I swear implacable hatred against all enemies of our Holy Roman Catholic religion, the only true one."[11] However the counter-revolutionary societies never gained the importance of the Carbonari, whose numbers in 1820 have been

estimated as between 300,000 and one million. It was the dominant liberal influence until the 1830s, when it was overtaken by the Association of Young Italy (*La Giovina Italia*) formed by Mazzini.

Revolutions of 1820

Ferdinand I of the Two Sicilies realized that the aims of the Carbonari were revolutionary, but wholly underestimated the numbers involved, and did nothing; while the Carbonari infiltrated into positions of power and penetrated his army. On 2nd July, 1820, hearing of a revolution in Spain, they persuaded General Gugliemo Pepe to lead them. They achieved a bloodless revolution and demanded a constitution and parliamentary government, which Ferdinand was forced to accept.

In October 1820 Metternich called a Congress of the great powers at Troppau. He drew up a protocol, or draft treaty, which stated that Austria had the right to intervene in Naples in order to preserve the peace. Then, after a plea for aid from Ferdinand, he sent an army to Naples, which easily overcame the rebels in March 1821. The new parliament was dissolved and its deputies went into hiding. General Pepe was forced to leave the country and Ferdinand executed leading Carbonari.

In the same week the Carbonari, supported by many army officers, took advantage of the departure of the Austrian troops from neighbouring Lombardy for Naples to lead a revolution in Piedmont. They demanded a constitution, and wanted Piedmont to lead the opposition to Austria's dominance in Italy. The King of Piedmont, Victor Emmanuel I, was unable to choose between granting a constitution, which might lead to war with Austria, and refusing, which would result in civil war. He thus abdicated in favour of his brother Charles Felix, who was thought to have liberal sympathies. The rebels delayed and failed to pursue their advantages, until Metternich sent 15,000 troops to crush them at the battle of Novara.

Novara

One of Italy's future heroes, Mazzini, recalls an incident at the time: "One Sunday in April 1821, while I was yet a boy, I was walking in the Strada Nuova of Genoa with my mother . . . The Piedmontese insurrection had just been crushed; partly by Austria, partly through treachery, and partly through the weakness of its leaders." The local people had seen the suffering of the revolutionaries, who "seeking safety by sea, had flocked to Genoa, and, finding themselves distressed for means, went about seeking help to enable them to cross into Spain."[12]

The fleeing rebels made a deep impression on him. "That day was the first in which a confused idea presented itself to my mind – I will not say of country or of liberty – but an idea that we Italians could and ought to struggle for the liberty of our country . . . the idea of an existing wrong on my own country, against which it was a duty to struggle, and the thought that I too must bear my part in that struggle, flashed before my mind on that day for the first time, never again to leave me."[13]

Giuseppe Mazzini left univerity in 1827 and wrote political articles. He
Mazzini helped to collect money and arms for the Carbonari, but soon became disillusioned with its limited aims: "In my own mind I reflected with surprise and distrust that the oath which had been administered to me was a mere formula of obedience, containing nothing as to the aim to be reached, and that my initiator had not said a single word about federalism or unity, republic or monarchy. It was war against the government, nothing more."[14]

In 1830 he was arrested on suspicion of conspiring against the Piedmontese state. When his father protested about this imprisonment without trial, the Governor of Genoa declared "Your son is a young man of some talent, and he is too fond of walking by himself at night deep in thought. What on earth has he to think about at his age? We do not like young people to think unless we know the subject of their thoughts."[15]

In prison in Savona fortress Mazzini was given ample opportunity both to think and to read. He was allowed four books, and his choice was significant: the Bible, which condemns injustice and oppression; the history of Rome by Tacitus, which told how the liberty of the people had been the glory of the state; the poems of Lord Byron, which were full of the spirit of revolt against tyranny; and the works of the patriot poet Dante, who saw as if in a vision the future greatness of Italy. These books convinced him that he had a mission from God to deliver his country from oppression.

20   During his imprisonment Mazzini formed the idea of the

Giuseppe Mazzini in his study at Brompton, in London, during his exile

Association of Young Italy. He was determined that it should be less vague and more positively national in outlook than the Carbonari. In 1831 he was exiled and, in Marseilles, founded the Association which was to revive patriotic feeling among Italian youth. With devoted followers he worked with an enthusiasm which stirred a quick response at home. Pamphlets were smuggled into Italy in barrels of pitch and bales of drapery. The words of Mazzini thrilled their readers: "Climb the hills . . . sit at the farmer's table, visit the workshop and the artisans, whom you now neglect. Tell them of their rightful liberties, their ancient traditions and glories, and old commercial greatness

*Association of
Young Italy*

21

which has gone; talk to them of the thousand forms of oppression, which they are ignorant of, because nobody points them out."[16] Lodges grew up in the chief towns of the north and centre, enrolling thousands of recruits. By 1833 the Austrian government considered "Young Italy" sufficiently dangerous to declare membership of it punishable by death.

"Education and insurrection"

Mazzini gave general instructions to members of Young Italy. Section Three of these said their objectives were Unity and a Republic. In unity rather than division lay strength, and he felt that only in a republic could free democratic government be ensured. Section Four stated that the movement intended to reach its goal through "education and insurrection, to be adopted simultaneously, and made to harmonize with each other."[17] Mazzini believed that "Italy is strong enough to free herself without external help; that, in order to found a nationality, it is necessary that the feeling and consciousness of nationality should exist; and that it can never be created by any revolution, however triumphant, if achieved by foreign arms."[18] Insurrection, to Mazzini, meant the organization of guerrilla bands to undertake irregular warfare as the first stage of a revolution against the monarchy and Austria. Rules for their conduct stated: "The essential weapons are a musket or rifle with a bayonet, and a dagger. Each soldier will carry his cartridge-box, a case containing bread and spirits, a thin but strong cord, a few nails, and, if possible, a light axe. The clothes worn by the soldiers should be so made as to allow of rapidity of movement, and of a shape not calculated to betray them in case of dispersion."[19]

The Duties of Man

In a collection of essays entitled *The Duties of Man* Mazzini expounded his theories. *The Rights of Man*, written by Tom Paine, an Englishman living in America, had strongly influenced revolutionaries in other countries, but Mazzini felt that the individual's responsibility to society, rather than what he might demand from it, should be emphasized. Man's duties were first to humanity, then to his country and his family. Only in a nation were the individual and humanity ideally united. Before true liberty could be achieved, Italy must become a nation. "The individual is too weak, and humanity too vast. 'My God,' prays the Breton mariner as he puts out to sea, 'protect me, my ship is so little and Thy ocean so great!' And this prayer sums up the condition of each of you, if no means is found of multiplying your forces and your powers of action indefinitely. But God gave you this means when He gave you a country, when, like a wise overseer of labour, who distributes the different parts of the work according to the capacities of the workmen, he divided humanity into distinct groups upon the face of the globe, and thus planted the seeds of nations . . ."[20] Countries should also respect each other's natural boundaries: "Bad governments have disfigured the design of God, which you may see clearly marked out . . . by the courses of the great rivers, by the lines of the lofty mountains, and by other geographical conditions . . . Natural divisions . . . will replace the arbitrary divisions sanctioned by bad governments. The map of Europe will be remade. The Countries of the People will rise, defined by the voice of the free, upon the ruins of the countries of Kings and privileged castes. Between these Countries there will be harmony and brotherhood . . . To you, who have been born in Italy, God has allotted, as if favouring you specially, the best-defined country in Europe."[21]

"The design of God"

From exile, where he spent the greater part of his life, Mazzini expounded his beliefs and worked relentlessly for his aims. Unfortunately, however, he was too inexperienced in the ways of the world and too mystical to put many of his ideas into practice. Although the moral effects of "Young Italy" undoubtedly aided the cause of unity, it did not succeed as a revolutionary body. A series of attempts were made to incite revolts, but wholesale arrests prevented them from making any progress.

One unsuccessful revolt, influenced by Mazzini, was planned by the Venetian brothers, Attilio and Domenica Bandiera. In 1842 they founded a Venice branch of "Young Italy." They had few followers – most Venetians were more interested in a revival of their own old republic than in a unified and republican Italy. The Bandiera brothers, however, were prepared to die for the cause, considering it a stain on the family honour that their own father, an admiral in the Austrian navy, had been responsible in 1831 for the imprisonment of Italian patriot refugees.

The Bandiera brothers

On 11th June 1844 the Bandieras sailed to Calabria, in the far

23

south, with fifteen companions, to free the people they insisted were fellow Italians. Before they left they asked Mazzini to tell their countrymen, if they fell, "to imitate our example, for life was given to us to be nobly and usefully employed, and the cause for which we shall have fought and died is the purest and holiest that ever warmed the heart of man . . ."[22]

Betrayal After their landing in Calabria, one of their number betrayed them. "They wandered for a few days in the mountains, looking for the insurgent band which they had falsely been told was waiting for them, and then fell into an ambush prepared by the Neapolitan troops. Some died fighting; nine were shot at Cosenza, including the Bandieras. The Corsican whom they suspected of treason . . . was condemned to a nominal imprisonment; when he came out of prison he wrote to a Greek girl of Corfu, to whom he was engaged, to join him at Naples, that they might be married. The girl had been deeply in love with him, and had already given him part of her dowry, but she answered 'A traitor cannot wed a Greek maiden; I bear with me the blessing of my parents; upon you rests the curse of God.' "[23]

The marytrdom of the Bandieras made a deep impression abroad, particularly in Britain. It had come to light that their correspondence with Mazzini had been tampered with in the English Post Office, and that their plans had reached the Austrian and Neapolitan governments through the British Foreign Office.

Austrian government Austria was one of the major European powers, and competed with Prussia for domination of Germany, which like Italy was divided into many tiny states. Although Austria proper was German-speaking, 80 per cent of the population of the Empire were members of the subject races – Magyars, Czechs, Poles, Rumanians, Serbs, Croats and Italians, most of whom remained under Austrian rule until 1918. Lombardy and Venetia were the responsibility of a Viceroy resident in Milan, but as in the other territories major decisions had to be referred to Vienna. Administration was centralized on a ridiculous scale; Venetians were amused that even soldiers' boots had to be sent from Venice to Vienna to be cobbled. Italians could not emigrate or even travel abroad unless, after endless questioning and delays, Vienna granted permission.

24

Hungarian soldiers keep constant watch on the frontiers of the vast Hapsburg Empire

The constant surveillance of the private lives of those unfortunate enough to come to the notice of the Sbirri (political police) was widely hated. Mazzini counted the numbers involved in this in Lombardy: "... 300 police agents, 872 gendarmes, 1,233 police guards, with a whole army of guardians, under-guardians, gaolers, *secondini*, guards of fortified places, etc ... There are spies of the Viceroy, of the Governor, of the Director of Police, of the Commissaries ... acting independently of each other, but all joining the main root of the Supreme Police at Vienna."[24] Feuds existed between rival local officials, fostered and encouraged by Vienna as a policy of "divide and rule" made it easier to keep all real authority there.

Though Lombards and Venetians liked the general conditions of law and order, the ample entertainment activities and commercial prosperity, because the government was foreign it was regarded by the patriots as more odious than the tyrannies of

A police state

25

Rome and Naples. The Austrians tended to be condescending towards the Italians and called the rich northern plain their "Lombard milch-cow." Italians were excluded from the higher grades of the civil service. Under Napoleon Italy had been considered part of a cosmopolitan Empire, whereas now its people were treated as a subject race. Mazzini pointed out: "In Lombardy there are *Germany* and *Italy*: that is to say, two races, having nothing in common – neither origin, nor language, nor manners, nor literature, nor belief, nor vocation; that is, a race of conquerors . . . and a race of subjects; that is, two distinct and hostile elements, which nothing, as is admitted on both sides, has been able to fuse together."[25]

"Nothing in common"

Austrian rule did have its good points. Education, and also justice, except in poltical cases, were better than in central and southern Italy. The civil service was honest, if excessively officious. The censorship of literature was no worse than in the other states, though strict compared with modern times. Though they were kept out of the higher army posts, the navy was not only manned but very largely commanded by Italians.

Marsimo D'Azeglio, born of a distinguished Piedmontese family, and later Prime Minister, found more freedom in Milan than in his native Turin. "The total absence of every symptom of energy and life, which oppressed me at Turin, could not be compensated for even by the pleasure of seeing my many friends and relatives . . . I felt literally stifled; and . . . had to return to Milan in order to breathe freely. And why? Because of the subtle art with which the Austrian authorities . . . contrived to soften and tone down the orders from Vienna . . . From 1840 to 1845 there were days at Milan of a rule so mild, so little terrorist, that every one of the petty governments of Italy has in turn proved itself to be infinitely more unbearable than the Austrian."[26]

Two Sicilies

In the South, covering three-eighths of Italy, lay the Kingdom of Naples and Sicily, the "Two Sicilies." In traditions, ambitions, character and social life the island and the mainland were most dissimilar, held together merely by the fact of common government; a bitter feud existed between Neapolitan and Sicilian.

In theory the state had the most enlightened code of justice in

Italy but in practice the King or his Police frequently ignored this when necessary to protect Bourbonists or to persecute liberals. Subjects, whether free or prisoners, sometimes experienced terrible cruelties, and the gaols, though official regulations were good, were described as "gulfs of hell."

The capital, Naples, then the largest city of Italy with over 300,000 people, was the spoilt child of the government. While peasants died of hunger, large sums were spent on the San Carlo theatre, and after 1830 large state grants were paid to the urban poor. "There was a traditional understanding that the Bourbons should leave the paupers of the slums to their idleness and crime, if they supported it when necessary, to intimidate the respectable and progressive classes. The *lazzaroni*, or beggars, numbered at least 40,000; a demoralized, idle mob, hardened by suffering . . . ready at a call to massacre artisans and tradesmen, and loot in the interests of church and throne."[27]

Naples

The Bourbon kings did little to improve the state of the nation, and seemed to take a fiendish delight in ruling like absolute tyrants. The following is considered a characteristic story of Ferdinand II, who came to the throne in 1830. "On the occasion of a popular festival in the piazza before the royal palace in Naples, the King was standing on the balcony, the Crown Prince, then a child, at his side. The boy looked out across the mass of people gathered below. Thinking of the high position he, in all probability, would be called upon to fill, he turned suddenly to his father and asked:

'What could a king do with all these people?'

'He could kill them all,' answered Ferdinand.

'He could, but he does not – because of his respect for holy religion.' And so saying he bowed low, and made the sign of the cross."[28]

"He could kill them all"

A Neapolitan priest, Giuseppe Campanella, described Ferdinand II as "quick of perception" but this "was entirely without cultivation, and, surrounded by counsellors who represented the least tendency to free thought as dangerous, he, 'to secure his own safety and power,' lent himself to the most guilty and brutal excesses."[29]

Corruption and dishonesty pervaded the central administra-

27

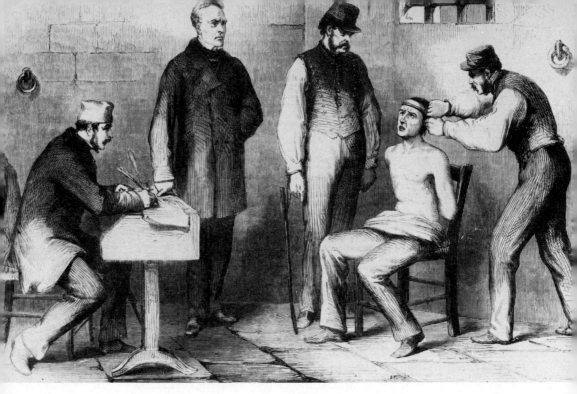

The use of torture on a political prisoner in the Kingdom of the Two Sicilies

tion and affected also the law, local government and education. Captain Charles Forbes, a former British Officer who later fought with Garibaldi, relates how officials in collusion with contractors squandered public money for their personal benefit. Though he refers to 1860, just after Garibaldi had taken over, it reveals the corruption which had existed for years. "For instance, A, a very disinterested commercial traveller, arrives from Marseilles with 30,000 shoes, and offers them at really a remarkably low figure to Garibaldi. The latter is delighted with the *Corruption* chance of having his army well shod, and sends him to B, the Secretary of State. B sends him to C, whose peculiar department it is. C remarks that they are too cheap, and he is sure A cannot afford to sell them at that price; thereby astonishing A, who imagines he knows something about his own business, and insists on selling at the original price. C ultimately dismisses him on some frivolous pretext. A calls again and again; and at last, anxious to get rid of his shoes and be off, bluntly demands what

C is driving at, when C tells him that if he will add £500 to his little bill, the State will trade with him. A, in desperation, agrees, and C draws on the treasury for the price of the boots plus £500, which he does not present to A."[30]

Crime was also seen to pay. "Crime was the surest means of attaining the highest dignities, and plunder was considered the most legitimate and honourable way of enriching oneself. Poor people have often heard from their fathers or their grandfathers that such a such a family, now so prosperous . . . was once very poor . . . and that they owe all their fortune to brigandage. The temptation therefore was great, and many a one . . . gave way to the fascination held out by the hope of being with little trouble rich and powerful."[31] Successful brigands became generals, knights and barons. Their strength "was founded on that system of fear which the authorities so freely employed. In a country suffering from the worst effects of misrule, men, reckless and unprincipled, but bold and energetic, associated in bands to carry out in town and country a system of terrorism similar to that which the government exercised over them."[32] *Brigandage*

The Camorra, an organization of the Neapolitan underworld, in return for controlling the poor and criminal classes, was allowed to fill positions of power within the police force itself. "They had chiefs in the twelve districts of Naples, in every town of the kingdom, and in every battalion of the army. They reigned unopposed wherever they considered it worthwhile to exercise their secret and irresponsible authority. They levied a tax on the fare of your cab-driver. They watched the markets and had their part of the profits, and in every gambling-house they gathered a contribution from the winner."[33] *The Camorra*

Crime was moderated by a certain moral justice. "The bandit, who was merciful to the poor, and attacked only the rich, found everywhere accomplices and adherents. Sometimes, when dying of hunger, he was succoured by the indigent, his brethren. It occasionally happened even that the country people practised brigandage as a trade, and made no secret of it in the presence of the military authorities.[34]"

A Neapolitan prefect found fault with a peasant who had not paid his taxes: " 'What can I do?' replied the peasant; 'There is nothing doing on the high road – I am out on it every day with my gun, but nobody passes. I promise, however, to go every evening, until I have picked up the fifteen ducats you want.' "[35] The natural inclination of the people towards brigandage was further favoured by geography, the lack of means of communication and the impenetrable woods and forests. Governments were slow to introduce improvements; lack of roads made travelling, even if it were safe, in most places impracticable; travellers without an escort rarely ventured anywhere. Those compelled to undertake a journey used, as the best guarantee of safety, an escort from the brigands themselves. There is a story of one voyager who took a guide in whom he had complete trust to ascend the mountains of Matese. "On passing a cross the guide declared 'This was placed here by me.' Then came the following conversation: 'By you! And for what reason?' 'It's a vow, Eccellenza.' 'A vow. May I ask its cause?' 'Why, it was for a certain misfortune which befell me on this very spot.' 'What do you mean?' 'I killed a man.' "[36] This information was not calculated to reassure the traveller. Before they left the mountain his guide had shown him no fewer than twenty-nine crosses, which he confessed had all been planted by himself for similar vows.

The Papal States   The Papal States rivalled Naples in misgovernment. Mazzini called the Papal government "organized anarchy," the worst in Italy: "The ecclesiastics, holders of the principal offices, incompetent from past habits and studies to undertake their administration, discharge their duties by the aid of inferior employees; these in turn, feeling their position uncertain, as dependent on a necessarily short-lived patronage, are guilty of every possible fraud, and aim solely at self-enrichment. Beneath all, the weary people, borne down by all, reacting against all, are initiated into a corruption the example of which is set by their superiors; or avenge themselves as they may, by revolt or the dagger."[37] At the head of all this was the Pope, spiritual head of the Roman Catholic Church but the equivalent of a king in Central Italy. A Pope might try to improve the conditions of his own people, but as a rule he was not close enough to the day-to-day administration to have much chance of success.

The traditions of the area around Rome were autocratic,

Many of the old, crippled, and unemployed in Rome lived off charity provided
by the monks

conservative and agricultural. "No man could be more peaceful
and unpolitical than the peasant of Umbria; he was perfectly
satisfied to till his small plot with its corn and vines and olives,
and to live, marry and die in the same way as his father and grand-
father before him."[38] But Romagna, further north, influenced
by Venice and Milan, was republican, liberal, commercial and
almost self-governing. Conflict between the two made the Papal
States the most unstable political unit on the peninsula. The
inhabitants of Romagna "were much given to conspire and rebel;
but these conspiracies and rebellions were nipped in the bud by
a system of espionage and terrorism quite unique – a system
in which were united the temporal and spiritual powers. Anyone
suspected of liberal thought in religion or politics was hunted
down, not so much by means of the police as by means of the

31

priests. The confessional was a ready way of obtaining the secrets of every family; and aged or dying persons were refused absolution unless they betrayed the haunts of their suspected friends and relations. The information thus obtained was grossly abused, and men were dragged before the Inquisition, tortured and imprisoned on the pretext of heresy, who were perfectly orthodox . . .''[39]

Inquisition   In 1846 a pamphleteer complained that the police "can imprison a man, banish him, exercise surveillance over him, refuse him a passport, confine him to a district, deprive him of civil rights, rob him of office, forbid him to carry arms or to leave his house at night. They open his letters in the post, and make no effort to conceal it. They can invade his house and seize his papers, they can close shops and cafes and inns, and fine us at their pleasure."[40] Political suspects at Rome were confined to their houses between sundown and sunrise, and driven to confession once a month. There was special surveillance of what a police document termed "the class called thinkers." Exiles from the Papal States were living penuriously abroad. Less fortunate victims were languishing in the Spielberg prison fortress or in the Sant' Angelo at Rome. Censorship was severe: "The Jesuits forbade the study of Dante in their schools; private circles to read economic books were banned, and the great bulk

The Index   of Italian and foreign publications were excluded. Most modern books of high repute and most newspapers were placed upon the Index of Prohibited Books. Of English papers, *The Times* was 'suspected,' . . . and in general all the Protestant and Tory papers that were adverse to religion."[41]

The poverty of Rome contrasted with the splendour of Papal ceremony. No commerce existed except tourism, and there was much begging and violence in the streets. The railway and the telegraph had not been allowed to reach the city, although by the 1840s they were becoming commonplace in the rest of Europe. Rome had the reputation of being the filthiest city in Italy except for Naples. There were fines for throwing garbage out of windows, but they were widely ignored. There was no street lighting; the sewers were open to the air, and cholera and typhoid, the diseases

32   borne by filth, were rampant.

2 The Revolutionary Years:
   1845–48

LUIGI CARLO FARINI, a Tuscan patriot, after the failure of a revolt in the Papal States, in 1845, wrote a document known as the Manifesto of Rimini. It appealed to the nations of Europe to force the papal government to carry out reforms which the major powers had suggested to Pope Gregory XVI in 1831. The manifesto was a useful restatement of the abuses of papal rule. It demanded an amnesty for all political prisoners, reform of civil and criminal law to conform to general European practice, the establishment of elective municipal councils, the admission of laymen to civil, military and judicial offices, modification of the press censorship, and removal of foreign troops. It was ignored.

Vincenzo Gioberti was a liberal Turin priest who had been asked to leave Piedmont because of complicity in Mazzini's unsuccessful plot in 1833. In his book *On the Moral and Civil Primacy of the Italians* he advocated a confederation of states united under the presidency of the Pope. "Mainly because of religion, Italy possesses within herself all the necessary conditions for her national and political rebirth, and to achieve this in practice she has no need of internal revolutions, nor of foreign invasions or imitations . . . That the Pope is naturally and must be the civil head of Italy is confirmed by the history of many centuries."[24] Nonetheless the elected Pope might be a foreigner, and the idea of a president with no knowledge of Italian affairs was not widely liked.

The Pope to lead the revolution?

The book, however, helped awaken public consciousness. It pleased the moderates who believed that Italy's problems should be solved by peaceful reforms instead of violent revolution, and

33

impressed King Charles Albert of Piedmont and Cardinal Mastai-Ferretti, Bishop of Imola, the future Pope Pius IX (*"Pio Nono"*). However many dismissed Gioberti's ideas as utopian, for while a liberal Pope might be elected, Austria would never give up Lombardy–Venetia without a struggle.

"Hopes of Italy"

In the following year another influential work, *Hopes of Italy* by Count Cesare Balbo, a Piedmontese aristocrat, also favoured the idea of a confederation. He hoped, unrealistically, that Austria would withdraw voluntarily, perhaps in exchange for increased territory in the Balkans (which would have involved war with the Serbs and Turks). He argued that the Pope was the wrong choice for leader, since if a war of independence became necessary the Pope would not lead Italians against Catholic Austria. For leadership he looked to Piedmont: "That worthy House of Savoy which had upheld the sacred flame of Italian virtue for the last century and a half," which had doubled its territory during that time and trebled its population "all at the expense of the House of Austria, and yet for the most part by fighting for them."[43]

In 1845 D'Azeglio, prompted by the Manifesto of Rimini, decided to travel through the Papal States to sound out public opinion and assess what support Piedmont could expect in a showdown with Austria. After the tragedy of the Bandiera brothers, he found that men were willing to discuss other methods: "The inefficacy, nay worse, the danger of acts which only serve to deprive the country of its best men, and to render foreign influence more harsh, has at last struck the most reasonable Italians; and there is a general yearning for a new life and system."[45]

"King Wobble"

D'Azeglio concluded from his journey that there was general keenness to fight Austria but little confidence in the Piedmontese king, Charles Albert. He tried to appear as a benevolent despot, but in practice avoided making firm decisions, and was known as "King Wobble" (*Il Re Tentenna*). Thus when D'Azeglio attended a private audience with him at 6 a.m. one autumn morning, in an attempt to find what support could be hoped for from the monarch, he expected only vague words of sympathy. The King surprised him with a firm statement of commitment to the liberals:

Charles Albert ("King Wobble") is welcomed by the people of Genoa in 1847.
Notice the reforming slogans on the banners.

"Tell these gentlemen to remain quiet and avoid a rising, as
nothing can be done at present; but let them be certain that when
the time comes, *my life, the lives of my sons, my sword, my
exchequer, my army, shall all be expended for the Italian cause.*"[45]
In 1848 the King was to honour these words, but at the time
D'Azeglio wrote "these are the words: God alone sees the
heart."[46]

In 1846 D'Azeglio published a small book, *Recent Events in
Romagna,* denouncing its misgovernment and its brutal secret
police. He advised Italians to indicate in a peaceful way at every
opportunity, verbally or in writing, their dislike of foreign or
arbitrary rule. He considered this form of agitation to be the best
method of securing free institutions and driving out the
Austrians. "This conspiracy in open daylight, with its own name

35

written on the brow of everyone, is the only kind useful, the only kind worthy of us . . . in this manner I incite every good Italian to conspire."[47]

Pio Nono   When Pope Pius IX was elected in 1846, he immediately revealed a degree of enlightenment by granting within a month of his election an amnesty to all political prisoners. "To all our subjects now actually in a place of punishment for political offences, we remit the remainder of their sentences, provided that they shall make in writing a solemn declaration that they will never, in any manner, abuse this favour, but that they desire faithfully to fulfil all the duties of good subjects."[48] He then formed a Council of State and started an enquiry into the need for reform. Plans were made for extending education, improving prisons, building railways and providing street lighting. The laws were reformed and the different courts coordinated. A State Assembly was formed, with delegates from provincial administrations. The creation of a civil police was permitted, and increased freedom given to the press.

A reforming   The Papal concessions aroused great enthusiasm in Italy. The
Pope   amnesty was interpreted not only as a sign of mercy, but also as an indication of political progress. The problem was that the Pope was torn between conflicting obligations. His first loyalty was to his position as Head of the Catholic Church. In his coronation oath he had sworn to hand on the church as he received it; this meant he could not give up its temporal power. Secondly he had a duty to the people of his state. This he could carry out by way of his liberal reforms. Lastly he felt a duty as an Italian to his country. His aim here was to follow Gioberti's ideas and to become the leader of a possible confederation which might develop from a customs-union, as appeared to be happening in Germany. Each state would maintain its independence, except that Lombardy–Venetia might at length be peacefully extracted from the Austrian Empire.

The Pope's most important contribution to unity was the stimulus his actions gave to national movements and liberal reforms in the rest of Italy between 1846 and 1848. Grand Duke Leopold of Tuscany soon introduced a civil police and a parliament, and similar concessions followed in Piedmont. As the

Romans read Pius IX's pronouncement of a liberal constitution

movement for liberty became stronger, the Pope realized that his own position in the Papal states was weakening, and that many of the liberals were working against him. In 1872, a saddened and embittered old man, he described what he had felt in the early years, when large crowds came to honour him: "Many came. I am convinced that they came in good faith. But even then from the deepest abysses of Hell, even then there was being prepared a way to overturn the world. And while these processions were becoming too numerous, and while I was urging, commanding and wishing for them to all return to their own daily work, the order of the day sent out from Hell was this: agitate and go on agitating always, because in troubled waters we may obtain our objects."[49]

"The order from Hell"

As a loyal Italian Pope Pius was hostile towards Austria, which had sent troops to occupy the city of Ferrara in the Papal States after local disturbances in 1847. However he was not prepared to do what Charles Albert urged on him, to preach a crusade against Austria and bring Italy behind him in a war of liberation. He was wildly popular – crowds in many towns and villages

37

chanted *viva Pio Nono* as a libertarian war-cry. But, in October 1847, Metternich summed up his dilemma. "Each day the Pope shows himself more lacking in any practical sense. Born and brought up in a liberal family, he was formed in a bad school; a good priest, he has never turned his mind towards matters of government. Warm of heart and weak of intellect, he has allowed himself to be taken and ensnared . . . in a net from which he no longer knows how to disentangle himself, and if matters follow their natural course he will be driven out of Rome."[50]

Conferences   The growth in the number of national academic conferences in the 1840s helped to increase the sense of unity among Italians. They were held in various cities of the north, but attracted delegates from all over the country. Problems of science applied to agriculture and industry were discussed, as well as the general economic and political future of Italy. In the Scientific Congress in Venice in 1847, Daniele Manin was active in the agricultural section. One day there was a debate on the potato disease. An Austrian policeman reported to his chief: "As in Italy the words for 'Germans' and 'potatoes' (*tedeschi* and *patate*) are equivalent and synonymous, you, sir, can well imagine that witticisms abounded, and if I had to accuse anyone, I should have to accuse the whole room. However it was all said sotto voce, in whispers and without scandal. Only Prati, coming down the steps, said to his friend, 'In our country only the Tedeschi really like potatoes: I wish they would go and eat them in holy peace in their own countries, and not dirty our fields with this disgusting vegetable. I am beginning to hope they will soon be gone.' "[51]

*Repression in   In 1846 Charles Albert embarked on a mild anti-Austrian
Piedmont*   policy, enforcing discriminatory tariffs on imported Austrian goods. However he showed no sign of making reforms similar to those in the Papal States. On 1st October 1847, the king's birthday, a crowd singing Pius' hymn was broken up by police with fixed bayonets. This official violence was bitterly resented, and a young man named Domenico Carbone wrote a satire on the king's policy of sometimes encouraging the liberals, sometimes attacking them:

> *"Swinging and rocking*
> *How pleasant it seems;*

Rocking and swinging,
A motion of dreams.
A little bit faster!
Slower . . . now more;
Pleasantly upwards
And down as before."[52]

The king was depressed to read the young man's verses and to find that they revealed his people's feelings about him. He was persuaded to introduce a few mild reforms, including a relaxation of press censorship and the transfer of provisional administration to new elected councils. One important result was the foundation of three newspapers, including *Il Risorgimento,* edited by Count Camillo Cavour and Cesare Balbo.

1848 was the year of revolution. Rebels, sometimes workers, frequently with middle class intellectuals in the lead, attempted to seize power in major cities throughout Europe. The February revolution in France brought down the Orleanist monarchy; for four months Paris was in the hands of the liberals, and the republic they established survived four years. There, and in Germany, the revolutionaries were demanding greater political freedoms from inefficient arbitrary governments. In the Austrian Empire, the subject peoples, Magyars, Czechs and Serbs, wanted above all increased independence from Viennese rule. In Italy a number of city revolts, inspired in the first place by a desire for greater local independence, soon linked together to become a national revolution. Municipalism, in the sense of the Italian's historic feeling of pride in his town or city, thus became one of the instruments of unification.

Year of
Revolution

The year began with the Tobacco Riots in Milan, a prosperous city increasingly discontented with the restraints on trade imposed by the Austrians. Reducing the use of tobacco, which was heavily taxed, would deal a severe blow to Austrian finance, so an appeal went out to the Milanese to give up smoking for the New Year. Marshal Joseph Radetzky, the veteran Austrian commander stirred up trouble by reacting violently. "On the first two days of January the streets of Milan were almost innocent of smoke, and the few who appeared with cigars were hooted or hustled. The military saw their chance. Huge distributions of

Tobacco Riots

cigars were made to the garrison, and officers and soldiers puffed their abundant smoke in the faces of passers-by. When the grim joke was resented, Radetzky showed his teeth. Cavalry charged at the unarmed crowd; workmen returning to their homes were bayonetted; several citizens were killed, over fifty wounded. Milan replied with one voice to the outrage; even the nobles and civil servants could keep silence no longer; high officials protested or resigned, and the Archbishop prayed in the Cathedral that their rulers might learn humanity."[53] Six months previously Radetzky had written to his daughter, "We look tranquilly in the face of a threatening future, we are universally hated, but we go on our way without caring about it."[54]

Marshal Radetzky [margin]

In February Luigi Torelli, a Lombard, described the situation: "Events are being precipitated by the brutality of the police and the ferocity of Radetzky ... Four months ago I could never have believed that hatred could spread everywhere so fast. The police are desperate and we are expecting them to confiscate arms ... The army of spies has been doubled. People live in continual fear of being arrested even on the lightest excuse. All hopes are now concentrated on Piedmont."[55]

In March a revolt broke out in Vienna, causing Metternich to flee the city. In Milan between 18th and 22nd March fierce rioting broke out. The Viceroy fled, the Municipal Council assumed control of the city, and barricades were hurriedly built. "In the rich quarters they used carriages, expensive furniture, elegant sofas, beds, mirrors; in the business quarters barrels, bales of cloth, pumps, packing cases; in the poor quarters, the lowly broom, hen coops, small tables, anvils, benches ... near the theatres, machinery, thrones, crowns, sham trees and sham giants; at the post office and under the archives, bastions of stamped paper and documents; wherever possible trees or shrubs were felled across the openings ... then the whole was completed with faggots, shutters, doors, paving stones, beer bottles and dirt."[56]

Barricades [margin]

On 22nd March Radetzky wrote in alarm to the Austrian Minister von Fiquelmont: "It is the most frightful decision of my life, but I can no longer hold Milan. The whole country is in revolt. I am pressed in the rear by the Piedmontese. All the bridges be-

40

Austrian troops fire on the rebellious people at Brescia, in Lombardy

hind me can easily be cut, and I have no time for replacing them.
Similarly I have very little transport. What is going on in my rear
I just do not know. I shall withdraw towards Lodi to avoid the
large towns and while the countryside is still open."[57] Radetzky
and the Austrian army were all forced to retreat to the Quadrilateral.

When in 1848 he granted a liberal constitution, Italy began to *Charles Albert*
look to the King of Piedmont as its natural leader – he was anti- *grants a*
Austrian, his army was national not local in outlook, and he *constitution*
ruled the state with the most developed internal economy. The
Constitution granted by Charles Albert to the Piedmontese on
4th March 1848 became the fundamental law of the state of Italy
for a century to come. Its provisions included:

Article 5: The King alone possesses executive power. He is
the Supreme Head of State, he commands all
forces on land or sea; he declares war; he makes
treaties of peace, alliance, commerce . . .

41

Of the Rights and Duties of Citizens:

Article 24: All subjects, whatever their title or degree, are equal before the law . . .

26: Individual liberty is guaranteed . . .

27: The citizen's home is inviolable . . .

28: The press will be free, but a law will check its abuses . . .

29: All property, without exception, is inviolable . . .

30: No tax can be imposed or exacted without the consent of the Chambers, sanctioned by the King . . ."[58]

(The two Chambers, or legislative houses of Parliament, were the Senate, whose members were chosen by the King, and the Chamber of Deputies, elected by the people.)

Revolt in Sicily   On 12th January 1848 rebels in Palermo, capital of Sicily, defeated Ferdinand II's troops. The revolt, led by Francesco Crispi and Giuseppe La Farina, had as its aim independence from Naples rather than the unification of Italy. The King was forced to revive Sicily's 1812 constitution, on 10th February to extend it to Naples, and to grant an amnesty to political prisoners. In February, too, the rebels forced Grand Duke Leopold of Tuscany to grant a constitution, and in March the Pope reluctantly agreed to do likewise in the Papal States.

Piedmont takes the lead   On 24th March King Charles Albert of Piedmont decided to support the revolts in Lombardy and Venice, where Daniele Manin, a lawyer and agitator for home rule, was leading the struggle against the Austrians. "We go," said Charles, "to the aid of our brothers in Lombardy and Venetia, relying on the help of that God Who is so plainly with us, that God Who has given us a Pius IX, and Who has inspired Italy to work out her own redemption."[59]

Although the Italian sovereigns were jealous of the King of Sardinia and Piedmont as leader of a national enterprise, and feared lest his popularity should strengthen the wish for a union of the states and deprive them of their crowns, they were compelled by the will of their people to support him against the common foe. Ferdinand II of Naples sent a force northwards

42

under General Pepe, but gave orders that they were to take the longest route and delay the march as long as possible. Leopold of Tuscany, as an Austrian, disliked making war on his countrymen, but he also found himself obliged to send troops to the front. Parma and Modena sent reinforcements. Pius IX allowed the Papal troops to set out for the frontier under the command of General Giovanni Durando. Every soldier, by the General's orders, wore a cross upon his breast, and they called themselves Crusaders, as taking part in a holy war. "Pius IX," said Durando, *Holy War* "has blessed your swords, united with the sword of Charles Albert."

Unfortunately Charles did not get all the help he needed. Though some of the aristocratic members of Lombardy's rebel government wanted union with Piedmont, Carlo Cattaneo and the democratic party were against annexation. Cattaneo believed that Austria would never again recover her lands, and that outside help was therefore unnecessary. Also he feared that Piedmont could not be converted to a fully democratic system of government. His aim was a confederation of the existing Italian states.

Then two of Charles Albert's possible allies, Papal States and Naples, deserted him. The Pope's clerical advisers warned that *The Pope* if the campaign proved successful, Charles would probably unite *deserts the* all Italy under his rule and the Papal States might be lost. More- *cause* over, it was awkward to quarrel with a great Catholic power like Austria, which had always shown itself a good friend of the Papacy. On 29th April Pius IX published his *Allocution*: "Seeing that at present some desire that we too, along with the other princes of Italy and their subjects, should engage in war against the Austrians, we have thought it convenient to proclaim clearly and openly, in this our solumn assembly, that such a measure is altogether alien . . . We cannot refrain from repudiating, before the face of all nations, the treacherous advice of those who would have the Roman Pontiff to be the head and to preside over some sort of novel republic of the whole Italian people."[60]

On 15th May, the day the new Parliament was due to be opened, a revolt occurred in Naples led by liberal democrats who wanted further reform, to go beyond the constitution granted on 10th

43

February. The King's Swiss mercenary troops suppressed the revolt ruthlessly. Ferdinand now felt confident that he could take the road of reaction, and regained his autocratic powers gradually. The need to restore his authority, and the Pope's *Allocution,* gave him excuses for recalling the strong army that had been sent to the North. All but 2,000, whom General Pepe persuaded to go with him to Venetia to fight the Austrians, returned to Naples. 30,000 ducats had been sent by the King via secret agents as an inducement for them to obey his orders.

"King Bomba"

In September the King launched a full-scale military and naval campaign against Sicily, which had proclaimed its independence on 18th April. His ruthless bombardment of Messina earned him the nickname "King Bomba." Soon all liberties were crushed, and the new parliament rendered useless. The King had regained absolute authority in his kingdom, but the lessons the people had learnt from the revolt remained.

The Austrians now poured reinforcements into Lombardy–Venetia, and Charles Albert was overwhelmingly defeated at Custozza and finally in 1849 at Novara. Edmund Flagg, a military correspondent on Radetzky's staff, quotes Radetzky's

The people of Messina flee by sea as the town comes under fire from "King Bomba's" fleet

official bulletin which praises the Piedmontese King and his sons the Duke of Genoa and the Duke of Savoy: "the Piedmontese and Savoyards fought like lions; and the unfortunate Charles Albert threw himself into the thickest of the danger upon every possible opportunity. His two sons, also, fought with brilliant courage."[61] He describes one scene at Novara: "Throughout the whole battle they were in the midst of the enemy's bullets, and it was in vain that their generals strove to draw them off. The Duke of Genoa, monarch-elect [by the rebels] of Sicily, led his division on foot, after having had three horses shot under him; and the Duke of Savoy, the present monarch of Sardinia, fought in the front ranks of the combatants when he no longer had a division to lead. It was a terrible fight. You can form no idea of the storm of bullets and shells which crossed each other in their dread course. Before and around the spot on which Field-Marshal Radetzky was standing, the heavy twelve-pound shot ploughed up the ground, tracing deep furrows in one place, and cutting trees down like stubble in another. A shell struck an officer in the breast, and, exploding at that instant, struck down a man at the right and the left, and cut off the upper part of the officer's body in such a fashion that his frightened horse galloped off some distance, with the feet of the corpse in the stirrups!"[62]

Battle of Novara

When the position became hopeless Charles Albert sued for peace, but rather than accept the humiliating terms demanded by the Austrians, he then abdicated in favour of his son Victor Emanuel, Duke of Savoy, and fled to Spain. His last address to his generals was: "To the cause of Italy . . . my life has been dedicated. For that I have risked my throne, my life and that of my sons. I have not succeeded. I recognize that my person is the one obstacle to peace. Since today I have failed to find death on the battlefield, I make my last sacrifice for my country: I lay down my crown and abdicate in favour of my son, the Duke of Savoy."[63]

Charles Albert abdicates

That same night he left accompanied by only two attendants, masquerading as the Count de Barge. He was stopped by an Austrian picket and taken to the Austrian leader's headquarters. Count Thurn was the one Austrian commander who had never seen the Piedmontese King. He was not recognized and was permitted to leave. After four months of secluded life in Spain he

Left Franz Josef, Emperor of Austria, in 1848. He was to reign until 1916.
Right Victor Emmanuel, the new King of Sardinia, in 1848

died on 28th July 1849, broken hearted. At least he was spared from witnessing the humiliating and harsh terms of the armistice which Piedmont signed with Austria on 26th March 1849.

Revolt in Rome   In the Papal States the events in the north had been followed with wild excitement. The resentment which followed the Pope's Allocution finally forced him to flee to Gaeta in the Kingdom of Naples in November 1848, after his minister Pellegrino Rossi had been murdered and a mob had attacked his own palace, attempting to set it on fire.

Mazzini, who arrived in Italy just as resistance in the north was fading, was elected to the Constituent Assembly of the newly declared Roman Republic and became its leader.

Republic   The Proclamation of the Republic of 5th February 1849 had four clauses:

"Article 1:   The temporal government of the papacy in Rome is now at an end, in fact and in law.

Article 2:   The Roman pontiff will have every guarantee needed for the independent exercise of his spiritual power.

Article 3:   The form of government at Rome shall be that of pure democracy, and it will take the glorious name of The Roman Republic.

Article 4: The Roman Republic will enter into such
relations with the rest of Italy as our common
nationality demands."[64]

The most immediate foe of the new republic was France. The *The French* *join in* new president, Louis Napoleon, wanted to prevent complete Austrian domination of Italy after her victory at Novara. If he could restore the Pope, it would increase his influence in Europe and gain Catholic supporters at home. On 25th April 1849 a French army under General Oudinot landed near Rome, expecting only light resistance. However at their first approach they were defeated with 500 killed or wounded and 365 taken prisoner. The repeated rushes of the volunteers, who were described by a French officer as "wild as dervishes, clawing at us even with their hands," forced the French back.

In charge of the republican resistance forces was Giuseppe *Giuseppe* *Garibaldi* Garibaldi, a sea captain, adventurer, and staunch republican, born at Nice in 1807, who had seen 12 years of action as a freedom

A carnival in Rome under the Republic of 1848. Notice the man dressed up
as a mockery of a priest.

fighter in South America. In 1833, when a merchant seaman visiting Marseilles, he had been told about Mazzini's "Young Italy." He soon joined, and when doing national service in the Piedmontese navy in 1834 received orders to subvert his comrades and seize a warship when a Mazzini-planned rising in Genoa started. The police found out about this but he managed to escape in disguise before arrest. In his absence he was sentenced to death for treason.

The defence of Rome, which lasted for three weeks, was accomplished only by the suicidal fervour of Garibaldi and his legion of volunteers. In the end they were forced to admit defeat, and the Pope was restored under French protection. But one of the last acts of the Republican Assembly was to confer on Garibaldi complete power in the territories of the Roman Republic. During the next twenty years of the struggle for Italian unity he regarded himself as Roman General-in-Chief, until he was able eventually to hand over to Victor Emmanuel as king.

Escape On 7th August Garibaldi fled. His long journey took him across Italy from Ravenna to the shores of the Mediterranean. Every day he had narrow escapes from discovery. He recalled one adventure at the wayside inn of Santa Lucia: "I had sat down on a bench beside a table and fell into an uneasy doze, my head resting on my arms . . . As I looked up my eyes fell on the unprepossessing countenances of some Croats [Slav subjects of the Austrian Empire] who had invaded the inn. I laid my head down again on my arms without appearing to have seen anyone."[65] The daughter of the house recognized Garibaldi and, with great presence of mind, kept the sergeant of the Austrian troop so well amused that he left without noticing the seedy wayfarer. These soldiers were the advance guard of three thousand men sent to scour the country for Garibaldi. Nonetheless, he eluded them all and escaped to Tangier, from where he sailed for New York on 12th June 1850, but his wife, Anita, whom he had married in South America, died on the terrible trek across Italy.

Venice With the fall of Rome the revolutionaries were crushed, except in Venice, where Daniele Manin was holding on against great odds, inspired by widespread dreams of Venice's former great-

48

French troops sent to suppress the Roman Republic attack the Porta Cavellegiere

ness. In 1847 Manin had been imprisoned for making speeches in favour of unity at a Scientific Congress. The Governor of Venice, the Hungarian Count Palffy, had made himself personally odious to Manin and his fellow-citizens by saying "To go against the Italians with cannon does them too much honour. A stick is enough."[66] Manin caused him to regret these words. Speaking on the law providing for the poor in Milan he said " 'We at Venice have all that and better.' Palffy blushed at the unexpected compliment. 'We have it,' continued Manin, fixing his eyes steadily on the Governor, 'we have it, it is true, but in the law only, not in practice.' Palffy went from red to purple."[67]

When the rising began in 1848, Manin was released by the revolutionaries. He became their leader, seized the arsenal, and proclaimed the Republic of Venice. Defence of Venice, which included 120 small islands, was an impossible task, but Manin, assisted by the Neapolitan General Pepe, valiantly resisted the Austrians. At first the besiegers tried using explosive balloons, then they found a better technique for bombarding the city. "The cannon were dismounted from their carriages, and arranged on beds of timber with the breeches sunk in the earth, so as to give them an elevation of 45°. By firing high into the air greater range was obtained, and projectiles could be thrown into two thirds of

49

The first ever bombing raid – the Austrians attack Venice by balloon in 1849

the city – the regions of St. Mark's and the Arsenal remaining still out of range."[68] Fugitives from the onslaught moved to the homes of Venetians out of range of the guns, and gradually to the inner city, while the rebel volunteers tried to hold the outer *Campanella* defences. A Neapolitan priest who had come from the south as one of a volunteer force to help in the struggle for independence described one experience: "One of those nights when I was preaching not only, like Sant'Antonio, to the fishes, but also to the air, to the moon, to the insects, in the hope that my voice might reach the Austrians, Captain De Virgilio came up to me and whispered, so that no one else heard him, 'Campanella, Radetzky is listening; he is certainly there in front of us, at the outposts; he has come there on purpose.' Hearing this unexpected news, I directly determined to profit by it and without losing an instant I cried out at the top of my voice, 'Radetzky! Radetzky! Radetzky! General and champion of despotic and tyrannical power, and being this, worse than the most ferocious hyena, lay aside the idea of carrying out this execrable mission.' "[69]

Campanella's prayers were useless. The Austrian soldiers, many of them Czechs and Slavs, may have sympathized with the Italians, but they were professional fighters with a habit of obedience. The Austrians used to reply to verbal abuse by sending on the water bottles in which messages were enclosed. One directed to Campanella personally said "if I did not leave off shouting like one out of his mind almost every night to the soldiers of Austria, persuading them to desert, the moment I fell into their hands I should immediately be shot . . ."[70] This did not stop him continuing his appeals but as a precaution he obtained from a chemist "a pill of the strongest poison, capable of producing the desired effect instantly. This I fastened into the corner of the front of my collar, so that if the need for it came, I had only to bite the collar."[71]

Cholera and famine adding to the confusion and overcrowding, resulted in the final surrender in August 1849. Flagg records the event in colourful language: "All honour to Venice! Honour to her brave defenders – to her devoted Dictator – to her gallant General-in-Chief – to her iron-willed Assembly – to her long-suffering, ever-enduring, never-yielding nor revolting population . . . to her intrepid sons, 'dead for Italy,' who, like water, poured out their hearts' blood on the batteries of her defence – to her high-souled, patriotic and beautiful daughters. She has fallen – the proud Queen of the Adriatic!"[72]

Surrender

Radetzky promised an indemnity to all who had taken part in the defence of Venice, with the exception of Manin and thirty-nine others, who were exiled. The "forty" left on board a French steamer. Manin settled in Paris, giving Italian lessons to support his family.

Emilio Dandola, who fought for the republican cause in Lombardy and in the defence of Rome, gives his reasons for the failure of the Italian revolutions: "Insufficient military forces,

What went
wrong?

without a commander of genius; governments not even allied to
each other by a formal treaty, actuated . . . by the ambitions,
jealousies and interests of their individual states, more than by the
desire of ensuring the triumph of a cause, in which they could not
easily measure their own particular advantage; popular passions
run wild in the midst of newly acquired and but slightly guarded
liberties, offering, therefore, a free field for the manoeuvres of
all classes of republicans, encouraged . . . by the example and
influence of France; such were the conditions in which Italy was
placed in the middle of 1848, when the war with Austria was at its
height, and which led to the fatal result . . ."[73]

On the Austrian side discipline, esprit de corps and contempt
for the Italians gave Radetzky's troops unity, which they were
slowly to lose as Austria felt ever weaker in relation to Prussia
and Russia. On the Italian side moderates (many of them mon-
archists), unitarian republicans and federalists all desired
independence but since they had no further common goal, could
not agree on tactics. Gioberti's vision faded when the Pope fled,
and Cattaneo's idea of republican federalism failed to overcome
local pride and the idea of the city-state. The only schemes left
with any credibility were Mazzini's plan for a democratic republic, or unity in a constitutional monarchy under the King of
Piedmont.

3 Piedmont unites Northern Italy 1849–59

VICTOR EMMANUEL was a far more determined character than his father, though he inherited neither his good looks not his polished manners. He enjoyed telling this story against himself: "On one occasion I was on a shooting expedition in a country district where I was not well known. A woman came to the royal shooting-box with a basket of eggs, and a man, roughly dressed, was standing in the doorway, who took the basket and spoke kindly to her. To him the woman confided her great wish to see the King.

'I am the King,' said Victor Emmanuel, for it was he.

'Oh no!' cried the woman. 'I am not going to believe that tale. A charming pretty woman like the Queen would not dream of marrying such an ugly man as you!' "[74]

The King disliked the formal atmosphere of court life, and enjoyed roaming the hills with his gun, dressed in shabby clothes. An old woman who met him in his shooting suit exclaimed "What a shame it is that while they tax us poor folk so heavily they cannot afford to give Victor a new pair of trousers!"[75] One day D'Azeglio said to him " 'There have been so few honest kings in the world, that it would be a grand thing to begin the series.' Victor, looking at him with a smile, asked 'Have I to play the part of an honest king?' 'Your majesty has sworn to the *Statuto*, and has thought of all Italy, and not of Piedmont only. Let us continue in this path, and hold always that a king, as well as an obscure individual, has one word only, and by that he must stand.' "[76] The King liked D'Azeglio's title for him of *Rè galantuomo* (Honest King), and when he was asked to sign the

The Honest King

The three men who did most to create a united Italy – (left to right) King
Victor Emmanuel, Count Camillo di Cavour and Giuseppe Garibaldi

register of the census of Turin, he wrote, under the heading
'Profession,' '*Rè galantuomo.*'

Victor Emmanuel hated Austria and wanted to avenge his
father and the disgrace of Novara. "The crown of Sardinia" he
declared, "has fallen very low; we need glory, much glory, to
raise it up again."[77]

Count Cavour   The history of Italy from the collapse of the revolutions of
1848–1849 to the war of 1859 centres round the political life of
Piedmont, and in particular the work of Count Camillo Cavour
(1810–1861). Cavour was a rich aristocrat, financial expert and
shrewd diplomat, and at the same time a convinced liberal. He
was certain that economic measures could help to free and unite

Italy, since it was apparent that the two most advanced industrial nations, Britain and the United States, also had the most democratic forms of government. One of his contributions to his newspaper *Il Risorgimento* stated: "The new public life which is spreading over all parts of Italy cannot but exercise a great influence on its material conditions. The political resurrection of a nation can never be separated from its economic resurrection. A people governed by a benevolent monarch, advancing in the path of civilization, must of necessity advance in riches and material power. In all countries where no political progress has been made, since the overthrow of the feudal system, commercial industry has either never sprung up, or has not flourished, or even declined."[78]

In 1850 Cavour became Minister of Agriculture, then later Minister of Finance. He promoted commercial reforms with the aim of stimulating the economy, reducing government debts and reviving industry. A railway was built between Turin, the capital, and Genoa, the major port. The banking system was reorganized, and co-operative societies were set up to help farmers. Cavour obtained the money he needed to begin his reforms by tapping the resources of the Church: taxing ecclesiastical lands, secularizing land belonging to decayed monastic orders, and suppressing many religious societies. In 1852 he was made Prime Minister.

Economic progress

To Cavour it was essential that Italy should expel Austria, once and for all. However, the defeat at Novara had shown that Piedmont could not hope to achieve this alone. He therefore began to look to England and France, the two European powers with liberal-minded governments, for help. This was totally against the teachings of Mazzini, who, despite the military odds against Italy, felt that outside powers would necessarily pursue their own interests and so any revolt, if it was not to compromise itself, must come from within. The following anecdote illustrates Cavour's hard-headed single-mindedness: "When he was about six years old he was taken on a journey by post-chaise [a coach which carried fare-paying passengers]. On one stage the horses were unusually bad. The little boy asked who was responsible for them. He was told it was the syndic. He demanded to be taken to the syndic at once to get the postmaster dismissed."[79] In contrast, Mazzini is described as having been a tender-hearted,

Help from abroad?

55

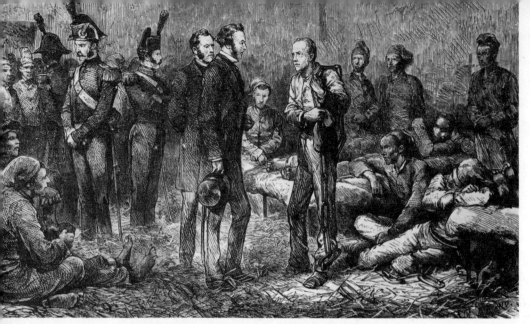

William Gladstone, future Prime Minister of Britain, visits political prisoners
in Naples

idealistic child: "When he was about six years old he was taken
for his first walk. For the first time he saw a beggar, a venerable
old man. He stood transfixed, then broke from his mother, threw
his arms round the beggar's neck and kissed him, crying 'Give
him something, mother, give him something.' 'Love him well,
lady,' said the aged man. 'He is one who will love the people.' "[80]

On 26th January 1855, Cavour signed an alliance with Britain
and France, and agreed to send troops to the Crimean War. The
decision appeared foolhardy – what had Piedmont to gain from a
war between Russia and the western powers? Cavour hoped,
however, that Italian participation would popularize the cause of
unification abroad – he could not expect more specific gains,
since Austria too was supporting the allied cause.

*The Crimean
War* Despite bitter opposition at home, 18,000 Italian soldiers were
sent to the Crimea, having heard Cavour's parting words: "You
have the future of the country in your haversacks."[81] The
response from a soldier in the trenches was: "Out of this mud
Italy will be made."[82] At the peace conference in Paris in
1856 Cavour gained the goodwill of the British and French but
no substantial benefits. The British were generally suspicious of
foreign involvement in Italy. "When someone asked Lord

Palmerston for a definition of the difference between 'occupation' and 'business,' he answered on the spur of the moment 'There is a French occupation of Rome, but they have no business there;' and this witticism correctly represented English opinion on the subject."[83]

Refugees

Many refugees from Lombardy, afraid of imprisonment for political offences, had settled in Piedmont. In 1855 the Emperor of Austria issued a decree declaring their property forfeit. The Piedmontese parliament voted a subsidy to recompense them. This increased Victor Emmanuel's moral stature, and republicans such as Manin and Garibaldi were now prepared to accept his leadership. In September 1855 Manin wrote a letter, also published abroad, of support for Piedmont: "Faithful to my flag – independence and unification – I reject everything opposed to it. If regenerated Italy must have a king, there must be only one, and that one the King of Piedmont. The Republican party makes a sacrifice to the national cause . . . It says to the House of Savoy: *Make Italy and I am with you. If not – no.*"[84]

The National Society

In 1857 Marquis Giorgio Pallavicino, a Milanese, and Giuseppe La Farina, a Neapolitan, helped to form the National Society. Its motto, "Italy and Victor Emmanuel," and its aim of unity under Piedmontese monarchy with a democratic system of government, were publicized throughout Italy in newspapers and pamphlets. Garibaldi joined, plus many of his followers, and Cavour gave secret support. The National Society soon had a wide membership among patriots in the Italian states. Mazzini remained outside it, planning further revolts in pursuit of his republican aims.

In February 1858 12,000 copies of the Political Creed of the National Society, written by its secretary La Farina, were circulated throughout Italy. "Here then is the noble and holy purpose of the National Society. We want to unify Italy, so that all the powerful elements which she embraces may co-operate in her liberation. We want harmony between ideas . . . between province and province, city and city, class and class. We want harmony among all genuinely professed religious beliefs . . . Finally harmony between the House of Savoy and Italy."[85] "Everything points irresistibly to political unification. Science, industry, commerce and the arts all need it. No great enterprise is possible any longer if we do not first put together the skill, knowledge, capital and labour of the whole of our great nation. The spirit of the age is moving towards concentration, and woe betide any nation that holds back!"[86]

Progress   The Political Creed makes it clear how much the desire for unity was influenced by events from abroad. People no longer expected the world to stay much the same as it always had been. They felt that it was expanding and getting better all the time – a spirit exemplified above all by the Great Exhibition of science and industry held in London in 1851. The frontiers of the known world were being extended by exploration and colonization, and new industries were offering a different way of life to the people of Europe. Italians, who felt that their country had been in the forefront of progress in the past, did not want to be left behind by new ideas and opportunities.

Napoleon III   It was to France that Cavour looked for most help against Austria. Louis Napoleon III, the French Emperor, had spent many years in exile in Italy as a young man. His elder brother had died fighting with the rebels in the rising of 1830, and Louis himself had been a member of the Carbonari in Romagna. However Louis' position as Emperor was precarious, so he was afraid of offending the French clerical party. Also he felt indebted to the Pope, who had once supplied him with false passports when he was fleeing for his life. He therefore delayed making any definite commitment to help the Italians.

Orsini   At this point Felice Orsini influenced the course of events. He was an Italian who had long been involved in revolutionary enterprises. In 1845 he had been condemned to the galleys for life by the Supreme Tribunal of Rome for conspiracy against the Papal government, but was one of those amnestied by the Pope in 1846. In 1849 he became a deputy in the Roman constituent assembly. The restoration of the Papal government obliged him to flee, and he sought refuge first in London, then Piedmont, Switzerland and Lombardy, everywhere concocting revolutionary intrigues, travelling with false passports, and hiding under false names.

In 1855 he was arrested in Vienna, where he was suspected of having planned an attempt on the life of the Emperor of Austria.

Napoleon III looks on as Orsini's bomb explodes among the bystanders

Imprisoned at Mantua, he was brought before a special court on a charge of treason, but he managed to escape in March 1856.

Describing his feelings while in prison, Orsini wrote, "How many families have not food to give their children! I languished in prison, but I know the reason why; but how many are free, who without any fault of their own, find none to help them! When I see the poor in the streets, I cannot forget my own sufferings from hunger and cold; and while I have a penny, I consider it my duty to help them."[87]

In London, a haven for many liberals exiled by autocratic governments, he was regarded as a respectable Italian political refugee. His book *The Austrian Dungeons in Italy* had been published by Routledge, and included the story of his daring escape from prison. It was dedicated to "those generous English hearts who labour unremittingly for Italy's freedom."

Then, in January 1858, Orsini threw bombs at the carriage of Louis Napoleon III as he was going to the opera with his wife. The carriage was riddled by no less than 76 projectiles; eight bystanders were killed, and nearly a hundred wounded, including many blinded, but the Emperor and his wife stepped from the carriage unscathed.

Orsini's bombs

59

When Orsini was brought to trial, Jules Favre, counsel for the defence, declared: "Gentlemen, the crime of Orsini was not dictated by greed, nor hate, nor ambition. What did he want? To free his country. He tells us so. Accuse him of folly, but do not question the honesty of his declaration; we have his whole life to prove it . . . He used his life unsparingly in an energetic incessant struggle against the enemies who oppressed his country. It could not be otherwise; hatred of the foreigner, gentlemen of the jury he had in his infancy from his mother's milk, his father's blood."[88]

Sentenced to be guillotined, Orsini addressed himself to Napoleon III. "As a simple individual, I dare to raise my feeble voice from prison, to beg you to give Italy again the independence that Frenchmen helped her to lose in 1849. Let me remind Your Majesty that Italians, including my own father, cheerfully shed their blood for Napoleon the Great, wherever he chose to lead them. Let me also remind you that neither Europe nor Your Majesty himself can expect tranquility until Italy is free. Do not scorn the words of a patriot on the eve of his execution. Deliver my country, and the blessings of 25 million people will go with you for ever."[89]

"Deliver my country"

The Orsini affair placed blame on the two governments with which Louis Napoleon wished to stay friendly – Piedmont, Orsini's birthplace, and England, where the bombs had been made. He was, therefore, unwilling to make too much fuss. Also he nursed a secret admiration for Orsini, the publication of whose letters from prison helped to persuade him that he ought to do something for the Italians. He therefore decided to meet Cavour. The failure of Orsini's assassination attempt thus achieved what its success would have made impossible.

Plombières

The meeting of Napoleon III and Cavour took place at Plombières, in eastern France, on 20th July. Cavour persuaded the Emperor to agree to an alliance, which was in fact a deliberate attempt to manufacture a war. France promised to supply 200,000 men to fight against Austria; on victory, Lombardy–Venetia and the Duchies of Parma and Modena were to be added to Piedmont. The Papal States and the Kingdom of the Two Sicilies were to form a confederation under the Pope.

Clothilde, daughter of Victor Emmanuel, was to marry Jérôme Napoleon, cousin of the Emperor. (This took place in September 1858.) France was to be given Savoy and Nice as the price for its help. The king at first opposed such terms, mainly because he did not wish his daughter to marry a rather dissolute man 21 years older than himself. Cavour persuaded him to win the war first, and argue about the terms later. The king agreed, and it only remained for Cavour to provoke Austria to fight without incurring blame as the aggressor.

The Treaty between France and Piedmont of January 1859, leading to an alliance in the event of war with Austria, provided as follows:

"Article 1: If aggression by Austria leads to war between the Piedmontese King and the Emperor of Austria, an offensive and defensive alliance will come into force between the Emperor of the French and the King of Piedmont-Sardinia.

Article 2: The aim of the alliance will be to liberate Italy from Austrian occupation, to satisfy the wishes of the people . . .

Article 4: Whatever happens in the war . . . the interests of the Catholic religion and the sovereignty of the Pope shall be maintained.

Article 6: The High Contracting Parties will accept no overtures for peace without previous agreement . . ."[90]

Terms of the treaty

Unfortunately, from Piedmont's viewpoint, Austria had no reason to want to fight a war in Italy. The propaganda of the National Society was thus directly aimed at infuriating her. Next, Victor Emmanuel, when he opened Parliament on 10th January 1859, made a provocative speech: "Our country, small in territory, has acquired credit in the Councils of Europe because she is great in the idea she represents, in the sympathy she inspires. The situation is not free from peril, for, although we respect treaties, we cannot be insensible to the cry of anguish (*grido di dolore*) that comes to us from many parts of Italy."[91]

Massari, a Neapolitan exile in Piedmont who was present at

Provoking Austria

the scene, said, "The speech was interrupted by clamorous applause and cries of *Viva il Rè*! But when the king came to the words *grido di dolore* quite indescribable enthusiasm was shown. Senators, deputies, spectators, all sprang to their feet with a bound and broke into passionate acclamations. The ambassadors of France, Russia, Prussia and England were utterly astonished and carried away by the marvellous spectacle. The face of the ambassador of Naples was covered with a gloomy pallor."[92]

The military forces in Piedmont were built up, and the National Guard enlarged and reorganized, to promote both fear and fury in Austria. Cavour sent for Garibaldi, and asked him to lead a new corps of volunteers. Cavour and Garibaldi had little in common, and in the opinion of the latter, "Count Cavour bore a lively resemblance to those noblemen of the *ancien régime* who looked down with disdain on the common people, and governed them accordingly."[93] In spite of his distrust of Cavour, however, he recognized Piedmont's usefulness, and hurried to Turin. Arriving at the palace of the Piazza Castello, he was ushered into the well-known Red Room, where Victor Emmanuel and

Cavour and Garibaldi

Cavour awaited him. "Well General," said Cavour, "the long-expected day is near at hand: we want you."[94]

Cavour continued, in his slightly cynical manner: "I have not an illimitable faith in the power of the insurrectionary

Volunteers leave Rome to fight for Piedmont in the war of 1859

element against the well-drilled legions of Austria. I think, moreover, that our regular army is too small to match the 200,000 men our enemy has massed on the frontier. We must therefore have the assistance of a powerful ally; and this is already secured."[95] Garibaldi is recorded as replying, "I feel that my first duty is that of offering my sword to my country. My war-cry shall therefore be 'Italian unity, under the constitutional rule of Victor Emmanuel!' Mind, however, what you are about, and do not forget that the aid of foreign armies must always be paid for dearly."[96] The king then took him by the hand and assured him that Louis Napoleon had always desired to see Italy free and happy, adding that he [the King] had only consented to the marriage of his daughter to Napoleon, because he was sure of the Emperor's good intentions towards Italy.

Garibaldi's warning

Giuseppe Verdi's music had already made the King a symbol of patriotic aspiration. Now *"viva Verdi,"* as the initials of *Vittorio Emmanuele Rè d'Italia,* was shouted in the opera houses and streets of Milan, and scratched on the walls, the Austrian authorities not realizing that it was more than an expression of musical taste. Lombards were gradually becoming enthusiastic about fighting on the side of Piedmont in a final showdown with Austria. Many fled from Lombardy and Venetia to Piedmont to evade conscription for the army, which Austria imposed at the end of 1858. Piedmont refused to extradite them. Some of these joined Garibaldi's volunteer force.

On 23rd April 1859 Cavour finally succeeded in provoking Austria into declaring war. The Austrians sent an ultimatum demanding that Piedmont should stop her military preparations within three days or face the consequences. This was ignored. On 26th April the war officially began, about one week earlier than Cavour, five months before, had predicted.

Austria reacts

At the start of the war Piedmont's position was perilous. It was a small country, with its best natural defence, the Alps, between it and its ally, France, and relatively open ground between it and its enemy. Its army totalled about 60,000, while the Austrians already had 100,000 near the frontier. However the aristocratic Hungarian Gyulai, commander of the Austrian forces, delayed assembling his troops in Italy, when he might have taken the

63

French troops ford the River Mincio, in Lombardy

initiative and defeated Piedmont before the French arrived. The first Austrian troops crossed into Piedmont on 29th April, but heavy rain held up their advance. They were further delayed since their commanders could not agree whether to make for Turin immediately or to attack Alessandria and the more vulnerable area to the south. By the time they had decided to march on the capital, French troops had begun to enter Piedmont, and the Austrians were pushed back across the Ticino river. The two allied armies were able to link up, and narrowly defeated the Austrians in two extremely bloody battles, at Magenta on 5th June and at Solferino on 24th June.

The Austrians hesistate

Battle of Magenta

Arrivabene described the scene at Magenta: "Trees thrown down by the dreadful effect of artillery; heaps of dead bodies in all directions; human limbs scattered about, together with carcasses of animals and military accoutrements . . . farm-houses burnt, crops trampled down, vineyards devastated, houses plundered; the churches, the houses, even the porticoes, filled with the wounded, the dead and the dying; such were the harrowing sights which met me at every turn." [97]

The Garibaldian volunteers played an important part in the fighting, compensating for their poor equipment by making better use of the rough terrain. Most of Garibaldi's officers were faithful friends who had fought with him before. However there were also adventurers from Germany, Switzerland, France,

A French colonel is shot dead as his regiment attacks the Austrians at Solferino

England, Spain, North and South America and even one Chinese. The most notable Englishman was Sir John William Peard. When about to start the campaign, Garibaldi had noticed coming towards him a tall thin man of about sixty, with a long white beard and carrying binoculars and a carbine. When they met, Garibaldi asked:

"Garibaldi's Englishman"

" 'Do you know what those who serve under me have to undertake to do?'

'No; but if you tell me, then I shall know.'

'No pay.'

'That does not matter. I am a rich man.'

'Ten leagues a day to march, on an average.'

'I have good legs.'

'Firing every day.'

'That is what I am on the look-out for.'

'Absolute obedience to my orders.'

'I would rather fight in my own way.'

'Ah! Good gracious, you want too much.'

'Very well,' said Sir John, 'I will fight on my own.'

'Fight on your own; you are right. It will be better to do so.' "[98]

The Englishman had the strange peculiarity of hunting the Austrians as if he were hunting the stag, the wild boar, or any other animal – just for the pleasure of hunting. Garibaldi loved a brave man, and on a later occasion said to Sir John in the thick

c

British volunteers bound for Sicily. Holding the binoculars is Sir John Peard ("Garibaldi's Englishman")

of the firing:

"'Sir John, I compliment you. You are a brave man.'

'I know that quite well,' was the Englishman's reply.

'And more than that, you are my friend.'

'Ah! That I did not know,' said Sir John, 'and I am very grateful to you . . . Pardon me, there is a devil of an Austrian who catches my eye.' Sir John put his carbine to his shoulder, and the Austrian who was attracting his attention was hit full in the chest, took three paces forward, and then fell on his nose . . . From that day forward, he was no longer called Sir John William Peard, but Garibaldi's Englishman.''[99]

Desire for peace After Solferino France and Piedmont were clearly winning. The war might nevertheless have continued for a long time, as the Austrians had retreated to the almost impregnable fortresses of the Quadrilateral. However Louis Napoleon and Emperor Franz Josef of Austria were now both anxious for peace. What were Napoleon's motives in contemplating an armistice before Lombardy and Venetia had fallen? He was shocked to witness the terrible toll of human life taken by the war, and the lack of medical facilities for the wounded. He was upsetting the Catholics at home by endangering the position of the Pope. He had wanted to see a Kingdom of Northern Italy as one of several states in the peninsula, but now the demands of Tuscany, Romagna, Modena and Parma for annexation to Piedmont indicated the growth of one large Italian state which would threaten the Papal States and perhaps also France's dominance in the Mediterranean. French financiers and industrialists were grumbling about the cost of the war. Above all the diplomatic situation was difficult. The other nations of Europe had no desire to see the balance of power upset. Prussia in particular hoped to exploit the war to gain supremacy over Austria in Germany, and warned France not to cross the river Mincio, the border between Lombardy and Venetia. Prussia was actually mobilizing, which alarmed both Franz Josef and Napoleon III, who had only 50,000 troops left in France.

Prussia mobilizes

Austria, too, wanted peace. She was undergoing an economic slump, and finding it hard to finance the war. Civil war threatened in Hungary, and troops had to be stationed there and in other parts of the Empire to keep order among the subject races.

Napoleon III, without consulting Cavour, suddenly concluded an armistice with Austria at Villafranca, near Verona, on 11th

Napoleon III toasts the French Army of Italy on their return from Lombardy after the armistice of Villafranca

July. The terms were:

*Armistice of
Villafranca*

"The two sovereigns support the creation of an Italian confederation under the presidency of the Pope.

The Emperor of Austria cedes to the Emperor of the French his rights over Lombardy except for the fortresses of Mantua and Peschiera . . . The Emperor of the French will then hand over these territories to King Victor Emmanuel.

Venetia will become part of the Italian confederation, though still belonging to the Austrian crown.

The Grand Duke of Tuscany and the Duke of Modena will return to their states, and will proclaim a general amnesty.

The two Emperors will ask the Holy Father to make certain indispensible reforms in his states."[100]

*"I will
become a
revolutionary"*

The news of Villafranca stunned the Italians. The Milanese were finally free of the Austrians, but what of Venice, Parma, Modena, Tuscany and the Papal States? It seemed a terrible betrayal. On 15th July Cavour described how Napoleon, who had promised to hunt the last Austrian out of Italy, had now solemnly left them in the lurch, and exclaimed, "If needs be, I will become a conspirator, I will become a revolutionary, but this treaty shall never be executed; a thousand times no – never!"[101] Cavour begged Victor Emmanuel to ignore the armistice and fight on. The king, however, felt there was no alternative but to accept it. Cavour resigned and went into seclusion for five months.

Although out of office, Cavour continued to give help and advice to the new moderate revolutionary leaders in the central states. These had taken advantage of the war in the north to overthrow their princes and establish constitutional governments.

In Tuscany the reactionary policies of Leopold II, otherwise a rather kind, bumbling man, compared unfavourably with the situation in Piedmont. Leopold took refuge with the Austrians in 1859, and it was announced by the provisional assembly that he would not be allowed back.

In Modena, Francis V continued the repressive rule of his father, filling his prisons with liberal political activists and his towns with spies. Count Carlo Arrivabene recorded extracts

The people of Florence demonstrate their support for the revolutionary government

from one of his essays found in the archives of Modena, proposing a federation of Austria and Italy. " 'With the concurrence of a powerful English fleet,' Francis wrote, 'we could easily land a powerful army on the banks of the Seine (!!!), *carry the French capital elsewhere*, and forever destroy the influence of that infernal nation.' It is not easy to make out what the writer really meant when he wrote these words; but by the Italian phrase 'Che la loro capitale venga trasportata altrove,' the idea of 'carrying Paris *elsewhere*' is fully conveyed [although *tra(n)sportata* is mis-spelt – Francis scarcely knew his subjects' language]. With such a headstrong man ruling a country despotically, it is not to be wondered at if the administration of the Duchy was in complete disorganization."[102]

The Mad Duke

In Parma there was a much-disliked regency, as the son of Carlo III, assassinated in 1849, was still a child. The majority of citizens were thus glad to be rid of their rulers, and influenced Romagna, the revolutionary part of the Papal States, to follow them in agitating for union with Piedmont.

Two talented leaders, Baron Bettino Ricasoli in Tuscany and

69

Luigi Farini who brought together Modena, Parma and the Romagna under the name of Emilia, united to oppose the restoration of the former princes. They were determined that the terms of Villafranca should be resisted, and the return of the old order made impossible except by force. They held out for unity with Piedmont, which the people wanted, and thus kept alive the nucleus of a united Italy.

Northern Italy united When Cavour, accepting Villafranca as perhaps a blessing in disguise, returned to office on 20th January 1860, his first task was to annex Tuscany and Emilia. Despite Napoleon III's continuing opposition, Victor Emmanuel accepted the four crowns of central Italy (little Lucca being the fourth). "The King of Sardinia, as he was still called, now had eleven million subjects, and on his head rested one excommunication the more. The Papal Bull against all who had, directly or indirectly, participated in the events which caused Romagna to change hands, was published a day or two before the opening of the new Parliament at Turin . . ."[103]

Addressing the representatives of his widened realm, Victor Emmanuel said, "Our country is no more the Italy of the Romans, nor the Italy of the Middle Ages; no longer the field for every foreign ambition, it becomes, henceforth, the Italy of the Italians."[104]

Count Arrivabene, travelling to Turin on 2nd April, overheard the following conversation: "'What do you think of the excommunication?' asked Marquis Pepoli of a young priest who entered at Parma station the railway carriage in which I was seated. 'I think,' answered the priest, 'that the Pope has been very wrong; for there is no divine law which prevents people from getting rid of governments they do not like. Moreover, religion has everything to gain in going back to its former simplicity. St. Peter, and many of the Vicars of Christ who came after him, had, as you know, no temporal power to exercise.'"[105]

Napoleon claims his price As Piedmont had gained what she had aimed for, Napoleon now claimed Savoy and Nice, as promised in the original agreement. Both areas, which in fact had large French populations, realized that they would be more secure under French rule, and in the plebiscites which were held an overwhelming number voted for union with France. Thus the old Piedmont came to an end. With its Alpine outposts surrendered, the capital, Turin, was militarily indefensible. A monarchist historian ruefully proclaimed in Parliament, "Finis Pedemontii!"

If the new state was not to be permanently dependent on France, it was essential now to create a fresh Italy, preferably with Rome as its capital. The Piedmontese government had done as much as international opinion would allow. It was now the turn of the revolutionaries.

4 Garibaldi

THE VICTORY of the Franco-Piedmontese armies in the summer of 1859, and the demand for annexation by the Central States, roused great enthusiasm in Sicily. In particular discontent was rife among the more educated middle classes. Their aspirations were rather in the direction of freedom from the Bourbon monarchy than in that of Italian unity. They looked, however, for any means of release from the gross misgovernment of which they were the victims.

Sicilian aspirations

Luigi Settembrini, a Sicilian academic, suffered lifelong persecution for his political opinions. When only twenty-two, he was imprisoned for belonging to a secret society. His guard said to him, "You are a professor and I am an ignorant soldier, but I can teach you something. The worst enemies a man can have are pen and paper."[106] Settembrini's learning was the chief reason why he was regarded as dangerous by the Neapolitan authorities. In 1847 he had exposed their misgovernment and made a plea for unity in his *Protests of the People of the Two Sicilies*. In 1849 he was re-arrested and brought to trial for high treason. Defending himself, he wrote: "Freedom I love dearly. It is the right of an honest man, and if to love it is a crime, I confess myself guilty."[107] He was condemned to life imprisonment in Ergastolo, a fortress on a lonely island thirty miles off the south coast of Italy.

The friends of the political prisoners never abandoned their efforts for their release. The strongest influence was that of William Gladstone, later to be British Prime Minister, who once visited the Neapolitan prisons. Filled with horror and indigna-

European indignation

73

Opposite Giuseppe Garibaldi, liberator of Sicily and Naples, photographed in old age

tion, he published an account of his experiences and described the government of Ferdinand II of Naples as "The negation of God." At last Ferdinand tired of his perpetual unpopularity abroad, and in 1859, perhaps ashamed of his cruelty, ordered sixty-five of the most notable prisoners, including Settembrini, to be released.

Meanwhile the notorious Salvator Maniscalco, Director-General of Police for Sicily in 1859, devised new torments to break the resistance of the liberals. Alexandre Dumas, the French *Torture* novelist, described two of the most horrible: "The 'Cap of Silence' was a kind of gag of diabolical perfection; and the 'Angelic Instrument' . . . an iron mask which encloses the head, and, when put into operation by means of a screw, slowly compresses it until it is entirely crushed . . . I was also shown a pair of handcuffs which cannot be closed without piercing the flesh to the bone, however thin may be the wrist upon which they are put. They have also renewed that form of torture used in 1809 by the Spaniards against our soldiers: hanging by the wrist."[108]

With the beginnings of a revolt apparent, the Police under Maniscalco decided to force a crowd of people in the Strada di Macqueda in Palermo to shout support for the King of Naples: "A group of soldiers and *sbirri* [political police] then came along shouting 'Long live Francis II!' There was no response from the people. The soldiers . . . then surrounded a group of them, saying 'Shout 'Long live Francis II.'' Profound silence reigned. Then, suddenly, the silence was broken. A man threw his hat in the air, shouting 'Long live Victor Emmanuel!' He fell dead instantly, pierced by bayonets. Then musket, bayonet and dagger got to *Massacre* work. Two more were killed, and thirty, including women and children, were wounded."[109]

"The Neapolitan authorities now began a system which surpassed in its rigour and suspicion even what they had done before. The police suspected strongly that most of the young men of the noble families were implicated in a revolt which had failed, that they had given their money freely for the purchase of arms and ammunition, and that they were the real heads of the whole movement . . . But nowhere are conspirators as cautious, and nowhere is their organization more secret than in Sicily. It is a

74

natural consequence of a government based on bayonets and spies. It was therefore difficult enough to prove anything against the real leaders. But the Neapolitan government is not to be foiled in its schemes by a want of proof, so they singled out seven youths, all belonging to the first families, and ordered the police to arrest them."[110]

Victor Emmanuel and Cavour, however, did not desire to encourage a revolt in Sicily. Soon after the accession of Francis II in 1859 they had proposed an alliance with Naples against Austria, provided the young king would reform his government. Such an alliance would have indefinitely postponed national unity. Francis rejected this offer of friendship, preferring to ally himself with Austria and the Pope. The Austrians had announced their intention of disputing the annexation of the Central States, and Pius IX had declined to accept the loss of Romagna.

In April 1860 Victor Emmanuel, who knew the King of Naples was plotting against him, sent a last warning to his royal cousin: "Italy can be divided into two powerful states of the North and South which, if they adopt the same national policy, may uphold the great idea of our times – National Independence . . . But if you allow some months to pass by without attending to my friendly suggestion, your Majesty may perhaps experience the bitterness of the terrible words – too late."[111] He went on "If you will not hear me . . . the day may come when I shall be obliged to be the instrument of your ruin."[112] *Francis II receives a warning*

Francis was unlikely to receive aid from abroad, except from the Austrians. At the beginning of 1860 Lord John Russell, the British Foreign Secretary, had written to Mr Henry Elliot, British Minister at Naples, "You will tell the King and his Ministers that the government of Her Majesty the Queen does not intend to accept any part in the responsibility nor to guarantee the certain consequences of a misgovernment which has scarcely a parallel in Europe."[113]

Mazzini now helped to foster revolutionary activity among the Sicilians, who began to think not only of freedom from the Bourbons but of the possibilities of local autonomy within a wider national unity. Some of the younger aristocrats even began to hope for union under the King of Piedmont. Mazzini *Mazzini agitates* sent agents to Sicily, notably Francesco Crispi, a native of the island, a lawyer, journalist and future Prime Minister of Italy. Crispi concluded that Sicily was a more promising area for a revolt than either Rome or Venice.

A Sardinian paper, smuggled into Palermo, announced the formation at Genoa of a committee to aid the Sicilians. Rosalino Pilo, a Sicilian who had spent ten years in exile, returned on 10th April 1860. The Palermo revolt of 4th April had just been crushed by the Bourbon troops, and Pilo, to keep the revolution alive, announced in all the villages between Messina and Palermo that Garibaldi was coming. He was taking a risk, as Garibaldi had not yet made up his mind to lead an expedition to Sicily. Garibaldi, however, when he heard of the Palermo uprising, declared: "Italians! The Sicilians are fighting against the enemies of Italy and for Italy. It is the duty of every Italian to help them with money, arms, and especially with men. The chief cause of the misfortunes of Italy has been disunion, and the indifference one province showed for the fate of another. If we abandon the brave sons of Sicily to themselves, they will have to fight the mercenaries of the Bourbon as well as those of Austria and of the priest who rules at Rome. Let the people of the free provinces raise their voices in favour of their brethren who are fighting – let them send their generous youth to where men are fighting for their country."[114]

To Victor Emmanuel's attempt to dissuade him, Garibaldi replied, "Sire: the cry for help which reaches me from Sicily has touched my heart and the hearts of hundreds of my old soldiers. I have not advised the insurrectionary movement of my Sicilian brethren; but, as they have risen in the name of Italian unity, personified in that of your Majesty, against the most disgraceful tyranny of our age, I do not hesitate to take the lead of the expedition."[115]

Count Cavour felt keen anxiety. A successful revolution in the South would undoubtedly hasten the union of Italy. Should it fail, or should Garibaldi lose his life, it would be an appalling disaster for the country. And what chance had a thousand volunteers against the twenty or thirty thousand troops that were garrisoned in Sicily?

The rebellious people of Palermo, in Sicily, massacred by royal troops

On the night of 5th–6th May 1860, Garibaldi and some 1100 men (The Thousand) embarked at Genoa on two small steamers, the *Piedmont* and the *Lombardy*. Many wore the famous red shirt, of South American origin. The majority of Garibaldi's followers were students, independent craftsmen, writers, scholars, and middle-class professional men such as lawyers and journalists. This group always formed the backbone of Italian nationalism. The very wealthy mostly liked things as they were, the poor peasants took little interest in politics, and factory workers were then too small a group to be important. There were also a number of foreigners, including ex-officers from the British and French armies.

In a letter Crispi describes the landing at Marsala, on the west coast of Sicily, on 11th May: ". . . we were able to disembark everything without accident – men, ammunition and artillery – notwithstanding sharp firing from four Neapolitan ships. Had we arrived two hours earlier, when these ships were in port, or one hour later, when they returned, our vessels would have been sunk. We really owe our safety to a miracle."[116] In fact one of the Neapolitan commanders, Captain Acton, hesitated to open fire, for fear of hitting two British men-of-war, sent to protect the many British residents engaged in the wine trade at Marsala. Captain Acton believed (quite wrongly) that the British ships had been sent specifically to cover Garibaldi's landing. The redshirts were also lucky in that only recently a strong body of troops had been withdrawn from Marsala.

After the landing Garibaldi's force set off north-east for Palermo. On the 13th he announced that he was assuming the dictatorship of Sicily in the name of Italy and Victor Emmanuel. For many years some Sicilians did not know what Italy meant, and believed that L'Italia or La Talia was the name of the king's wife.

Garibaldi took the first step towards establishing his authority when he met the Bourbon troops at Calatafimi on 15th May. The position of "the thousand" was desperate – "Nino Bixio, the fiery commander of the first company, whispered in Garibaldi's ear, 'General, I fear we must retreat.' The chief started as if stung by a scorpion, but on seeing who it was that spoke, he answered

Freed prisoners in Palermo lead their former gaoler round the streets before shooting him

gently, 'Never say that, Bixio . . . Here we die!' "[117] Towards the end of the battle, Garibaldi and about three hundred men paused behind a stone wall to take breath, before making a final rush to a hilltop. "The Neapolitans at short range were trying to fire into them, and the Garibaldini pressed round their chief, asking for orders . . . As he sat resting, his head bowed on his hands, a clod of earth hit him full on the back. In an instant he leapt to his feet. 'Come on,' he shouted. 'They have spent their ammunition; they are throwing stones.' "[118] On the last rush the summit was reached, and the Bourbon troops forced to retreat to the nearest village.

Though over a thousand cheering Sicilian spectators had given noisy support, only about 200 had followed Garibaldi into battle. He now turned to one of his men, Giuseppe Bandi, and remarked, "You will see . . . that once we are seen to be winning, those who are now merely watching us will join our ranks."[119] Though Calatafimi was only a small encounter, it was very important in convincing many locals that Garibaldi's forces

79

Sympathetic priests help the people to demolish the royal fort at Castellamare, near Palermo

would eventually triumph, and gradually the Sicilian insurgent bands joined him. In a letter to the leader of one of these bands, Rosalino Pilo, on 16th May, Garibaldi wrote: "Proclaim to Sicilians that now is the great moment to destory the Bourbon regime, and we shall soon complete our victory. Any weapon will serve in the hand of a brave man – a musket, a scythe, an axe, or even a nail on the end of a stick. Join my forces and harass the enemy in any way possible. Try and have fires lit on all the hills around his troops. Shoot as much as possible at his sentries and advance posts by night."[120]

G. C. Abba, in his *Diary of one of Garibaldi's Thousand*, recollects the attitude of a local monk, Father Carmelo, when asked to join the cause:

" 'I should come, if only I were sure that you were on some great mission, but I have spoken with many of your comrades and the only thing they could say to me was that you wish to unite Italy.'

'Certainly we do, to make one great people.'

'You mean, one territory; as far as the people are concerned they are bound to suffer and they go on suffering, and I have not heard that you want to make them happy.'

'Of course! The people will have liberty and education.'

80

'Is that all?' broke in the friar. 'Liberty is not bread, nor is education. Perhaps these things suffice for you Piedmontese, but not for us here.'

'Well, what do you want, then?'

'War ... We want war, not war against the Bourbons only, but against all oppressors, great and small, who are not only to be found at court, but in every city, in every hamlet.'

'Well, then, war also against you friars, for wherever I go I see you have convents and properties, houses and fields.'

'Yes indeed. Also against us ... But with the Bible in your hand and with the cross before you – then I should join you; your aims now are too limited.'"[121]

A Sicilian noble who died in 1957, in his novel set in Sicily during the early 1860s, gives the impressions of an elderly aristocrat on discovering a dead Bourbon soldier. "The Prince remembered the nausea diffused throughout the entire villa by certain sweetish odours, before their cause was traced: the corpse of a young soldier of the Fifth Regiment of Sharpshooters who had been wounded in the skirmish with the rebels at San Lorenzo and came up there to die, all alone, under a lemon tree. They had found him lying face downwards in the thick clover, his face covered in blood and vomit, crawling with ants, his nails dug into the soil; a pile of purplish intestines had formed a puddle under his bandolier."[122]

Garibaldi's main strategic aim was to capture Palermo. Once inside he would rely on the local population rising in revolt to help him hold the city and drive out the remaining troops. The odds, however, seemed extremely uneven: "In the town were 20,000 troops, well equipped and provisioned, backed by four frigates and two forts; in the hills were a few thousand badly-armed peasants, and under eight hundred travel-worn redshirts. On this side, however, there was also Garibaldi."[123]

A column of 3,000 Neapolitan troops under a Swiss officer, Colonel von Mechel, was now sent to chase Garibaldi away. Garibaldi retreated, and von Mechel and the local people were fooled into believing that he was "on the run." In fact the retreat was a ruse to deceive the enemy as to his numbers and movements. He sent his wounded, sick and baggage into the interior,

"Liberty is not bread"

Tricking the Neapolitans

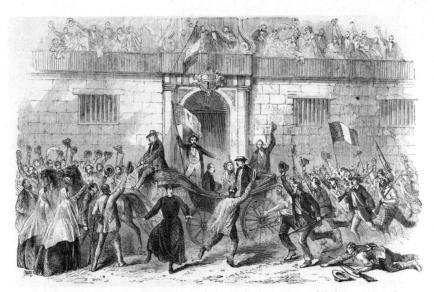
Freed political prisoners are cheered through the streets of Palermo. A priest and two nuns join in the celebrations.

while the main body of his troops turned suddenly east and under cover of dark doubled back along a rough path towards Palermo. Von Mechel followed the wrong column.

Garibaldi was at dinner in the village of Misilnieri when three American naval officers and a Hungarian called Eber, the correspondent of *The Times*, happened to visit him. Eber brought detailed information about the Palermo defences. The city was garrisoned on the outskirts, while the centre was free of troops. The weakest gate was the Porta Termini, on the south-east. Garibaldi decided to storm this and drive a wedge into the town centre. From there, helped by the citizens, he would fight outwards by means of barricades.

Garibaldi and his followers succeeded in forcing the gate, but soon had to contend with bombardment from the citadel and from frigates in the harbour, which did much damage and caused many casualties. One of the redshirts, the novelist Ippolito Nievo, gave this description: "I had a musket that fired only once in every four attempts, a loaf of bread spiked on my bayonet, and a fine cactus flower in my hat, with a splendid bedspread over my shoulders . . . Meanwhile we all ran in ones and twos like sheep, through alleys and squares, chasing Neapolitans, and also to stir up the Palermitans to revolt or at least to make them build some barricades. But we succeeded only indifferently, for the Neapolitans were too busy running away and the Palermitans seeking refuge from the indiscriminate gunfire which was now taking place."[124]

Armistice

After three days of street fighting the Neapolitan commander asked for an armistice. This was a stroke of luck for Garibaldi, because not only was he almost out of ammunition, but von Mechel arrived only a few hours later, intent on revenge for being misled into taking a false trail. He too, however, was bound by the truce.

General Fernando Lanza, the commander, on 3rd June received orders from King Francis to annihilate Palermo, but a loophole was left so in the last resort he could do what he thought best on the spot. Lanza wrote back to the King that his position in Sicily had become impossible, "that if he remained another week in contact with the insurgents his army would have disappeared, since all were disposed to desert his standard, and that the bombardment of the town was not only useless, but would probably encounter opposition from the consuls, and from the foreign admirals who were in the harbour."[125]

Garibaldi, as Dictator of Sicily, receives an ambassador from the King of Naples

83

Good relations with the local people became slightly strained when the Garibaldian volunteers hunted the Sicilian peasants' hens for breakfast

Palermo surrenders

The King then sent orders for a complete capitulation, which was signed on 6th June. The astonishing spectacle was seen of 20,000 soldiers marching out of the city to embark for Naples, in front of a handful of red-shirted men and civilians with antiquated weapons. At about this time a *Times* correspondent wrote: "Men of all classes, of all ages, of all parties, have only one business, one subject and one object – how to help Garibaldi. To live in Turin or Genoa, in Milan or Florence, and not to be Garibaldi-mad is impossible."[126] It was not long before volunteers of many nationalities were sailing to Palermo to help his cause.

Cavour takes an interest

Giuseppe La Farina was sent by Cavour to keep watch on Garibaldi, and ensure that Sicily was united with Piedmont and not made an independent republic under Garibaldi. In a letter to Cavour of 10th June, he described the conditions he found in Palermo. "More than one fourth of the city has been reduced to a heap of ruins ... In some places there is no trace left of the old streets, and from all these shapeless masses there issues a stench of decaying bodies that is sickening ... The city swarms

84

with people armed with guns, pistols, pikes, pruning-knives and spears. Many priests and friars may be seen among the armed throng, blunderbuss on shoulder and crucifix in hand, and they one and all preach the crusade against the Bourbons in the name of God and the country, and deify Victor Emmanuel."[127]

Sicilian vengeance

He described how the people were kind and generous to the Neapolitan soldiers, who since the capitulation were deserting in large numbers, but showed no mercy for the police. "When they discover the hiding-place of one of these it is difficult to prevent them from murdering him. Garibaldi makes every effort to prevent such acts of violence, and many owe him their lives, among others that famous Captain Chinnici, inventor of the *sedia ardente* (the burning chair) and other modes of torture that have filled Europe with horror."[128]

King Francis, while Garibaldi was in Sicily, appointed a new ministry to effect some liberal reforms, in the hope of winning back his people's loyalty. An able diplomat, Signor Manna, was sent to Turin to negotiate an alliance with Piedmont. Only six months before, this had been rejected contemptuously by Naples when it had been proposed by Piedmont. Now Cavour said it was too late, and that further negotiations were useless. Piedmont did not want to shoulder the guilt of an aggressive war, but Cavour knew that the cry of "Down with the Bourbons" was echoing throughout Italy.

Garibaldi still had to conquer the rest of the island, and the

Garibaldi's English Battalion takes part in the attack on the Citadel of Milazzo

Neapolitans had a strong force of 18,000 troops at Messina, barring the way to the Italian mainland. Francesco Crispi, one of "The Thousand," was left to form a provisional government at Palermo, while Garibaldi began to liberate more of the island.

Battle of Milazzo

Soon he was involved in a hard struggle with 4,000 royal troops at Milazzo. One of his foreign officers at this engagement was a Colonel Dunne, who had sold his commission in the British army to fight under other flags. If he was not obeyed quickly he took strong measures: "A Sicilian company, under fire for the first time, failed to show sufficient promptitude in executing an order to escalade a wall and jump into a garden, from which the enemy was keeping up a brisk fire. Dunne caught up half a dozen of the men into his saddle and pitched them bodily over the wall. The effect was singular, for, seeing the Garibaldians falling from the clouds, the Neapolitans took to their heels, exclaiming 'They can fly! They can fly!' "[129] Eventually, on 20th July, the Garibaldians won the battle. The victory, however, was an expensive one. The Garibaldians, now strengthened by local supporters and by further volunteers from abroad, lost 755 dead or wounded, as against 162 on the Neapolitan side. This was largely because at first the royal troops had a strong defensive position and were protected by artillery, an advantage which became useless once the Garibaldians penetrated their lines.

"They can fly!"

Marshal Cléry, commander of Messina, discouraged by the defeat of his best troops, the evident lack of morale among his men, and the vacillating methods of his King, signed a treaty suspending all hostilities in Sicily. Already on 13th July the King's ministers had vetoed a proposal to send some of the 80,000 soldiers on the mainland to recover Sicily.

Garibaldi was now in effective control of the whole island, and while his chief ambition was to cross the straits and liberate the mainland of Naples, he took care to reverse some of the worst evils of Bourbon rule. It was written thirty years later that

Garibaldi's dictatorship

". . . some of the old English residents in Sicily say that the island made more real progress during the few months of Garibaldi's reign than in all the years that have followed."[130] He introduced many interim measures to combat poverty. For

The revolutionary army lands on the forbidding mainland coast at Marina di Palmi, in Calabria

example "he had money and food distributed every morning to the most destitute, at the gates of the royal palace, where he lived with a frugality that scandalized the aged servants of royalty whom he kept, out of kindness, at their posts . . . he allowed himself a civil list of eight francs a day, and the day had never far advanced before his pockets were empty, and he had to borrow small sums from his friends, which next morning were faithfully repaid."[131]

Credit was also due to Garibaldi's chief administrator, Crispi. He was responsible for attempting to restore order, for with the removal of the authority of the Bourbons the old systems of police and the courts had broken down. He encouraged foreign trade, with the aim of making the new republic economically independent. In particular he passed laws to take care of all those families who had suffered loss in fighting for the national cause, and those who had earlier suffered ill-treatment under the Bourbons.

Many Sicilians now desired immediate annexation to Piedmont. This was seen as the best security against reconquest from Naples, and the quickest way to get a stable administration, even if not the republican one many of the rebels would have liked. Cavour too was in favour of annexation, and believed that his own agents in Naples would be able to start a revolt there without Garibaldi's intervention. Garibaldi, however, supported by Crispi, decided to retain his freedom of action until military operations were complete. They feared that if immediate

Union with Piedmont?

87

annexation took place and Sicily became Piedmont's responsibility, Cavour would prevent them from launching a military campaign on the mainland.

The way was now open to cross the Straits of Messina, two miles wide, to the Calabrian coast. Foreign warships could, however, prevent this. Napoleon III tried to stop Garibaldi's progress and the cause of Italian unity, which he now feared as a threat to French security, by proposing that Sicily be made into an independent kingdom under a prince of the House of Bourbon.

Britain takes Italy's side

But Lord John Russell, Foreign Secretary of Great Britain, the dominant naval power, refused to take any action against Garibaldi when Cavour's special agent told him that, though officially Piedmont disapproved of Garibaldi's activities, privately it supported them. On 27th July two letters arrived for Garibaldi from Victor Emmanuel. The first, intended also for France and the world to read, requested Garibaldi not to cross Straits; the second, intended for the general's eyes only, hinted that he was to do precisely that (though it is not certain whether the second letter was delivered).

Garibaldi ended his reply as follows: "As soon as I shall have fulfilled what I have undertaken by freeing the peoples from a hated yoke, I will lay down my sword at your feet and obey you for the rest of my life."[132]

Eventually Garibaldi and his followers crossed to the mainland without difficulty, leaving a provisional assembly to cope with the government of Sicily. The crossing was safeguarded by the presence of a British fleet, sent to discourage any intervention by the French or Austrian navies.

Garibaldi the invincible

Garibaldi's progress up the peninsula to Naples was a continual series of triumphs. Neapolitan soldiers, isolated by a hostile population and led by incompetent officers, were terrified of the redshirts. Count Maffei recalled that some "believed that, when in the thick of battle Garibaldi was struck by the enemy's bullets, he had but to shake the folds of his tunic to make them fall harmless at his feet."[133] This legend of invincibility contributed to his success. Sir Charles Forbes, one of his soldiers, described how Garibaldi exercised "an individual power over his soldiers wholly without parallel among modern commanders.

... With this imaginative race, their faith in their chief amounts almost to a superstition: whatever he says, is – wherever he appears, victory follows as a matter of course."[134] His striking looks, and pleasant unpretentious manner which enabled him to be equally at home in all levels of society, endeared him to thousands who saw him. In some villages in France and Italy his picture was kept framed in the golden shrine of a saint.

General Gallotti, Neapolitan commander at Reggio, was completely outmanoeuvred by Garibaldi on 20th August, expecting him to attack from the sea rather than the mountains. Arrivabene later heard him say, in explaining his defeat, "I am an old soldier, and so of course I expected Garibaldi to attack me in front, and he came from behind instead."[135]

Resistance collapses

Bixio, with the main column, stumbled upon outposts at the entrance to the city:

" 'Chi va la?'

'Garibaldi.'

'Avanti!'

It was the National Guard standing aside to let them pass. They hurried on through the sleeping streets. In the middle of the town they came upon other sentries.

'Chi va la?'

'Garibaldi.'

Bang!

They had come upon the loyal troops at last."[136]

Gallotti had placed his men in poor strategic positions in the town, and after a fierce struggle was defeated. During the battle "Bixio's horses received nineteen wounds, and their rider two in the arm, to which he paid no attention until Garibaldi sent him to bed the next night, saying 'I suppose the balls that reach you are made of puff-paste.' "[137]

On 5th September news reached King Francis that Garibaldi was approaching Naples. The King held a council of war to decide whether to remain and fight or to withdraw. Old General Carracosa said bluntly to the King, "Father, if you leave now, you will never come back."[138] The other generals, however, advised the King to leave Naples to save it from the damage that would be caused by a bombardment.

Garibaldi raises his hat to the people on his entry into Naples

Next morning Francis II's farewell proclamation was found posted in the streets. Part of it read: "We solemnly protest against this incursion of foreign troops, and We appeal to the justice of all civilized nations! The war is approaching the walls of the city. It is with unspeakable pain that We leave it, with a portion of Our army, in order to try to prevent, as far as lies in Our power, its injury or destruction . . . Should it please Divine Justice once more to reinstate Us to the throne of Our forefathers, all We pray is that We may be allowed again to see Our Neapolitans reconciled and happy."[139]

Both Cavour and Garibaldi were surprised by the loyalty of the Neapolitan army to the King, since they had assumed that the soldiers shared the feelings of the people as a whole and that if Garibaldi succeeded they would desert wholesale to support his cause. George Trevelyan, an English historian, states: "The loyalty of the soldiers was a measure of their professional feeling and of their isolation from the community at large, to whom they had been related not as defenders of the fatherland or representatives of the national honour, but as the tyrant's bodyguard kept to repress the citizens."[140] Half of them now rallied round

Stories were told of wounded prisoners being burned alive by the Neapolitan soldiers. The artist did not draw this scene from life, and the incident may have been invented as propaganda.

Francis II in his last-ditch stand against Garibaldi, while the rest disbanded, returning sulkily home or taking to the hills as brigands.

Everywhere Garibaldi was greeter with adulation. Arrivabene describes one scene: "The crowd streams slowly through the Toledo, on its way to the Palazzo d'Angri. Garibaldi has been obliged to appear on the balcony, and address the people, more than once. It is getting late, however, and the General has retired to rest. But how is it possible to sleep amidst the cries which rend the air? What is to be done?" The officers of the staff held a conference. One of them appeared on the balcony and, when he had quelled the clamour, said " 'The Dictator has gone to bed ... please do not disturb him.' From that moment, as if the whole multitude has been struck dumb, the people become silent; not a cry is heard throughout the Toledo."[141]

Garibaldi's welcome

The loyal troops of Francis II, stationed at Gaeta, made it doubtful whether Garibaldi's advance could make any further progress. It was at this moment, as Garibaldi began to establish his battle-lines in readiness for a confrontation on the River Volturno, that Cavour decided to let Piedmont take an official role in the drama. He wished to foil any further attempt by Garibaldi to remain as Dictator in the south, and at all costs to

91

Inside the fortifications at Gaeta, photographed on its capture in 1861

Cavour commits himself

prevent him from carrying the war to Rome, with all the international complications which that would cause. On 12th September, Cavour informed the powers of Europe that, for the sake of order, he was sending troops into the Papal States. On the 18th, the Piedmontese army under General Enrico Cialdini defeated the Papal army at Castelfidardo, and liberated all the Papal territories except Rome. Cialdini then pushed on into the Kingdom of Naples, where battle was raging along the river Volturno. The arrival of the Piedmontese turned the tide, and victory was achieved on 1st October.

Russell's Dispatch

Lord John Russell, the British Foreign Secretary, had in October 1860 sent a dispatch to all European powers stating clearly that Britain gave moral support to the Italian movement for independence as it was in the traditions of the "Glorious Revolution" in Britain in 1860. An Englishman in Italy observed that thousands of Italians copied it from each other, receiving it as a welcome victory in their national cause. One Italian statesman said that the dispatch was worth more than a hundred thousand men. It discouraged Austria, possibly backed by

Victor Emmanuel (left) and Garibaldi ride in triumph through the streets of Naples

Russia or Prussia, from planning any military intervention against the Piedmontese invasion of the Papàl states.

At the beginning of 1861 the bombardment of Gaeta increased. Because of the siege lack of food was becoming a problem. On one occasion "A Piedmontese shell exploded on the shore. It sent a great jet of water up in the air and cast four little silver fishes at the Queen's feet. On another occasion a shell fell into the water beneath one of the batteries. It threw a large fish on to *Siege of* the outworks. The fish was one which the Neapolitans call *Gaeta* *spinola* and which they consider a great delicacy. A sailor climbed down over the walls, seized the fish, and carried it up to the royal kitchen. The King and Queen accepted it with gratitude, as a welcome change in the daily fare, and the court were invited to dinner to partake of it."[142]

In February 1861 Gaeta fell and Francis II fled with his retinue to Rome. On 5th April he sent a circular to the rulers of Europe in which he "earnestly begged them to oppose everything which might come from the King of Sardinia, who had received his power from the hands of the revolution."[143]

On 4th October 1861, Garibaldi wrote to Victor Emmanuel *Victor* inviting him to come and receive the newly conquered territory. *Emmanuel* When the King arrived, on 26th October, Garibaldi resigned his *takes over* dictatorship and handed over the reins of office to him. It was Garibaldi, however, whom the crowd knew and adored. Alberto

A scene in a Naples polling-station during the voting for union with Italy

Mario, one of the Dictator's staff, who watched the meeting, said, "Garibaldi was at his wits' end to direct their attention from himself to the King, and, keeping his horse a few paces behind, he cried, with an imperious gesture, 'This is Vittorio Emmanuele, the King, your King, the King of Italy. Viva il Rè!' The peasants stared and listened; then, not understanding the tenor of his speech again shouted 'Viva Galibardo!' The poor general was on the rack, and knowing how dear to princes is applause, and how much his popularity irritated the King, would have given a second kingdom to wring from the lips of those unsophisticated boors an 'evviva' to the King of Italy."[144]

"Viva Galibardo"

Plebiscites were held in the liberated territories to make known the wishes of the people and prove to the rest of Europe that Piedmont had not simply made a conquest. The majority voted for unification. Marc Monnier, however, writing about the Naples plesbiscite, said: "Yesterday's promise that the vote should be free was honoured, nevertheless the method of voting left much to be desired. The ballot box was between two baskets, one full of *Yes* slips, the other full of *No* slips. An elector had to choose in full view of the Guards and the crowd. A negative vote was difficult or even dangerous to give. In the Monte Calvario district, a man who voted *No* with some bravado was punished with a stiletto blow – assassin and victim are now at the police station."[145] Thus the plebiscites were scarcely a serious test of public opinion.

Voting for unity

Giuseppe di Lampedusa, in his novel *The Leopard*, describes the mayor's study in the Sicilian village of Donnafugata after the local plebiscite: "Behind the Mayor's writing-desk gleamed a brand new portrait of Garibaldi; and (already) one of King Victor Emmanuel hung, luckily, to the right; the first handsome, the second ugly; both, however, made brethren by prodigious growths of hair which nearly hid their faces altogether. On a small low table was a plate with sone ancient biscuits blackened by fly droppings, and a dozen little squat glasses brimming with rosolio wine: four red, four green, four white, the last in the centre: an ingenious symbol of the new national flag."[146]

Many committed republicans who had fought in the war of liberation found it impossible to accept another king, even one who ruled constitutionally. It seemed unlikely that he would solve the south's economic problems, or give equality and justice to the poor. To one of his oldest friends who abstained from voting for this reason, Garibaldi declared: "You have done wrong. I have always been a republican, and am so still; but I understand the republic as the supremacy of popular will, in opposition to the single pleasures of the sovereign. The unanimous will of the Italian people is to unite under the sceptre of King Victor Emmanuel. I have done everything in my power to realize this wish, and so ought you to do."[147]

"Supremacy of popular will"

With his services no longer required, Garibaldi, refusing a dukedom, returned to the simple life on his farm. Nevertheless, with Venetia still unfree and the road to Rome closed by the French, he had no intention of giving up the struggle. In 1861, he formed the Society for the Emancipation of Italy. The final achievement of one of the goals of the Risorgimento, the uniting of all Italians under one government, seemed within sight. However, there was still much more to be done.

5 *Problems of Unity*
1861–71

ANNEXATION TO PIEDMONT did not by any means solve all the problems of the south. In many ways, unfortunately, it increased them. At the same time as enthusiasm was being expressed over national victory, other events were taking place which should have warned that not all the causes of the revolt could be resolved by a political gesture. The power of the landlords over the peasants was unchanged, and the poverty of the latter unrelieved. In many parts of Sicily "the peasantry rose in fury against landowners and the rich, to the cry of 'Down with the rats' ... Violence was put down with violence ... Absolutely nothing was done. The nationalization of church property was the only government action which might possibly have helped the peasants; but in practice it was merely a financial operation, designed to make money for the government itself, and did nothing to help the island's economy."[148]

No change in the South

There was total disagreement as to how and when things should be done. Constantino Nigra, from Piedmont, describes what he found on his arrival as Governor of Naples: "There is continual clamour; one side cries 'Hurry up with unification, destroy every vestige of autonomy, give the central government entire responsibility for local affairs.' The other side replies: 'Respect the traditions and institutions already in existence, keep all that is good in local administration, and do not turn away destitute all the old servants of the Bourbons.' "[149]

The main difficulty was caused by Piedmont's attitude to the south. The sudden death of Cavour in June 1861 left a tremendous gap in the Piedmontese leadership, and the officials sent to the south, the *consorti*, ignored the differences of tradition and way of life and pushed forward relentlessly to bring about the total absorption of Naples by the new Italian kingdom. A particular grievance was that the laws were modified to conform with those of Piedmont. Crispi, in a letter to Mazzini of March 1865, complained that no consideration had been given to the possible contribution that the Neapolitan laws could make to the new state. While Piedmont "staggered beneath a load of codes that dated back to the days of despotism," the provinces of Naples and Sicily were "in spite of that tyranny that had long held all freedom of thought in check, further advanced both as regards civilization and the perfection of their codes and administrations ... Thus with some slight alterations ... the legal regime of the southern states might be regulated to form a basis for the organization of the nation."[150]

The consorti

Many aristocrats, who had hoped for some measure of autonomy, and expected themselves to play some part in government, never reconciled themselves to northern domination and returned their support to the Bourbons and the Pope. "In almost every branch of the administration, the *consorti* changed the names without altering the reality; whilst, on the contrary, the secret of governing a new country, in such a manner as to obtain the confidence of all classes, is to change the old system without altering the names. In effecting these changes, too, instead of making them gradually and in such a manner as not to arouse the jealousy of the people, they were determined on and executed at once: without the slightest deference to the feelings of the Neapolitans, the central jurisdiction of Turin was increased, while Naples was deprived of much of that official authority which it once exercised."[151]

Baron Sidney Sonnino from Tuscany wrote about the *consorti* in Sicily: "We have legalized the existing system of oppression and guaranteed impunity to the oppressor. In present-day society, any legal tyranny is normally kept in bounds by fear of rebellion. In Sicily, however, our institutions are based on a merely formal liberalism and have just given the oppressing class a legal means of continuing as they always have. All power has been handed over to these people, to use or misuse as they

"We have legalized oppression"

97

D

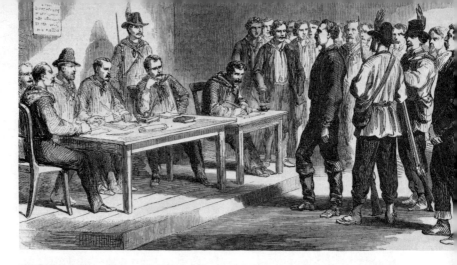

The trial of Santomeli, a Sicilian brigand chief, before a revolutionary Council of War

please."[152]

Added to these problems were the underlying differences between north and south. The north had better soil for agriculture, and more raw materials for industry, consequently a much higher standard of living, which was envied by the southerners. Few people in the south had received any education, and there was thus little pressure for social and economic progress except in response to particular grievances. Politics were still conducted conspiratorially, and there was little enthusiasm for commercial and economic projects.

Leopoldo Franchetti, a Tuscan aristocrat, wrote about the conditions of rural life in the Abruzzi, on the Adriatic coast: "Here the peasant depends on his landlord even for food. There is nothing of commerce or industry except for some shops and a few artisans in the towns, and hence the vast majority of people belong to one of the two classes: they are either landlords or farm labourers. The only way to escape is by emigration. What exists here is a system of real slavery, and not just economic slavery but personal bondage . . . Apart from rent, a peasant will almost everywhere pay contributions in kind, and will owe free services at the discretion of the lord. The landlord's crops are produced and carried for him by peasants who come for a longer or shorter time as they live near or far, and who will eat in his house while they do it."[153]

"A system of real slavery"

Discussing the changed political situation, Franchetti observed, "The normal constitutional guarantees mean little to the common people. Peasants who cannot write or read, and who know absolutely nothing of civil and political rights, can derive little advantage from freedom of the press or of association. Even where they are electors [illiteracy and tax qualifications meant that little more than one per cent of the population had the vote] they cannot use this right for their own advantage. Nor does religious liberty have any significance to a people which is without exception superstitious . . ."[154]

The right to vote?

The people of the south had to adjust to a new system of law. Many Piedmontese had only supported the *Risorgimento* on condition that their own laws and traditions should apply to the new state. They felt that any scheme for unity which allowed freedom to the regions would eventually break up, or play into the hands of corrupt local officials. Thus in November 1859 Piedmontese laws had rapidly been applied to Lombardy, and to other regions after 1860. The government thought it was a waste of time to study other systems and local preferences, but in many areas it seemed as if unity had imposed yet another foreign domination.

Economic, social and political grievances led to a revival of brigandage, which found favour among the Church and ex-Bourbon supporters. The exiled King Francis soon found himself involved in the schemes of the Legitimist Party in Rome, becoming the centre of a counter-revolution which, having no hope of victory by way of the ballot box, found its outlet chiefly in brigandage. Clara Tschudi, a Norwegian writer, describes how the brigands "from time to time, shouting cheers meanwhile for the dethroned King, made incursions into Neapolitan territory; but, as a rule, drew back hastily across the frontier, into the security of the Papal dominions; the great ladies of the Legitimist Party asked their friends among the officers to wink at the doings of the brigands, and consequently, when the French succeeded in capturing a few of these banditti, they handed them over at once to the Papal officials, who let them go on their way. The Queen-Dowager spent a large part of her fortune in supporting the brigands, who performed their feats

Brigandage

in the name of the royal family. Francis also gave all he could spare from the crumbs he had been able to save."[155]

The brigands were not merely seeking plunder, but also aiming to incite the people of the Two Sicilies to revolt by revealing the misery that Piedmont had brought. A Bourbon supporter, Giuseppe Tardio, went to Rome and put himself at the head of a band of criminals. In July 1862, without attempting to conceal his identity, he issued a proclamation: "To the People of the Two Sicilies. Citizens! The factious despotism of the Piedmontese government seduced you, at the conquest of the kingdom, with deceptive promises. You have reaped bitter fruits *"Loaded with* therefrom. This fair country is reduced to a province, you are *misery"* oppressed with taxes and loaded with misery and desolation."[156]

As an absolute monarchy, Naples had always been regarded as the surest supporter of the Pope's temporal power in Rome, and the Church still sought to exploit the fervent Catholicism of the south. Part of the Bourbon army which had taken refuge in the Papal States was used by Papal officials, such as Cardinal Giacomo Antonelli, for harrassing activities against Victor Emmanuel's new government in the Two Sicilies. The Pope, understandably, saw the Piedmontese as the real brigands, since they had recently taken most of his territory by force.

The Church supported all forms of opposition to the regime. Goaded in particular by the law nationalizing Church property, of which there had formerly been a great deal, "Members of the Neapolitan clergy first sought to favour the reactionary move- *The priests* ments, and then, when these were baffled and overthrown . . . *help the* they lent their aid to their natural heir – to brigandage. A single *brigands* word spoken by them from the pulpit, a single hint uttered in the confessional, would have sufficed to remove or at least to mitigate the scourge. But that word was not spoken; that hint was not given."[157]

Instead, brigandage was openly encourged. In December 1862, in the pulpit of a crowded church in Naples, the preacher said: "Our brethren, the brigands, are obtaining victories in different provinces of Italy, and will always obtain them, because they are fighting against an usurping king; the Virgin 100   cannot but perform the miracle of driving the usurpers from the

A Sicilian brigand confesses and receives absolution from a priest before being executed

kingdom."[158]

While the brigands were protected by the parish clergy, a Piedmontese might unofficially be seriously discriminated against. "Sergeant Romano, a brigand chief, was in the habit of having a mass celebrated by priests, whom he paid for their services . . . which was commonly known as "the brigand's mass," thus attempting to make heaven the accomplice of their crimes . . . In the very same province, a corporal of our army was lying on his death-bed, and the priest, when called to administer the consolations and sacraments of religion to a brave man who had fought the brigands, heartlessly refused them."[159]

"The brigand's mass"

The brigands were extremely superstitious. On certain days they would not eat meat, although they never refrained from murder and robbery. "In order to make themselves invulnerable, that they may be able to brave death with courage when about to enter on their bloody enterprises, they get themselves conse-

101

crated by a priest, who delivers to them the wafer of the Holy Sacrement, which, by means of an incision in the flesh, is inserted into the root of the thumb."[160] According to a General Villarcy, "They have litanies chanted in the woods, and they wear on their persons little images of the Virgin, and horns to protect them against the influence of the evil eye."[161]

Commission
of Enquiry

In January 1863 a Parliamentary Commission of Enquiry went to Naples. They came to the conclusion that brigandage was weakest in places where employer–worker relations were satisfactory, even though it was not specially against the local rich that the brigands' attacks were directed. Also conditions were better where labourers were not nomadic, but bound to the soil by ties of interest. But on large estates, where workers had little chance of knowing their employers personally, and there were too many workers attempting to make a bare living, brigandage became a savage protest against centuries of injustice.

The Commission advocated long-term measures of social reform. Its members had been to the country and seen its problems, but most of the deputies in the Piedmontese parliament had never visited the south, unless they were landlords there themselves. They wanted peace, but since most of them came from the upper class they were not prepared for such drastic measures as breaking up the large estates and giving land to the peasants.

Repression

Parliament, instead of trying to remedy the basic causes of revolt and unrest, attempted only to control their symptoms. The harsh and repressive Pica Laws were passed. "The government shall be empowered to confine under house arrest for anything up to a year any vagabond or unemployed person, or anyone suspected of belonging to the Camorra or harbouring brigands . . . In those provinces declared by royal decree to be infested with brigands, any armed band of over three persons organized for criminal purposes, and their accomplices, shall be punishable by a military court."[162]

More troops were sent to the south, and soon almost half the national army of 120,000 men was stationed in the Two Sicilies. More Italians, on both sides, died in the five years after the south

was united with Piedmont than in all the other wars of the

Risorgimento combined. Thus for most of the former subjects of the Bourbons unification meant martial law, a death in the family, and continuing desperate poverty and illiteracy. Many began to emigrate to seek prosperity in America. Brigandage continued, to take the modern from of the Mafia.

Emigration

Cala Ulloa, Prime Minister of the Neapolitan Government in Exile (supporting the Bourbons) reported on the state of affairs in Naples in July 1863. "Piedmontese troops are in occupation of southern Italy, but only thanks to a rigorous and pitiless enforcement of martial law. Under the old regime, before 1860, Naples could be placed under emergency regulations after an insurrection, but just for a matter of three days, and without people being arrested, without suspending freedom of the press. The Piedmontese, on the other hand, have kept Naples under martial law for six months; and Neapolitans are treated by them not as people fighting for their independence, but as slaves who have revolted against their masters."[163]

General Govone, after leaving his military command in Sicily, reported to Parliament in December 1863 that "there is an old, ineradicable prejudice by which Sicilians utterly despise the man who gives evidence against even the worst criminal. This attitude of silence has a special name among the common people – *omertà* or submission. Fear of possible vendettas is, alas, all too justified. Every day people were killed even in the centre of a town for suspicion of being in touch with the police ... This is a tremendous problem for Sicily. Since nobody will go to the ordinary courts for redress, everyone seeks his own method of self-defence."[164]

Vendettas

Before he died, Cavour started secret negotiations with Rome, hoping the Pope would voluntarily relinquish his temporal dominion. In a speech to Parliament in March 1861, he said: "Rome is the only city in Italy with more than purely local memories ... Rome, Rome alone, must be the capital of Italy ... We must go to Rome, but on two conditions: we must go there in agreement with France, and ... the true independence of the Pontiff must not be lessened. We must go to Rome, but civil authority must not extend its power over the spiritual order ... I am ready to proclaim in Italy this great principle: a free Church

"We must go to Rome"

in a free State . . ."[165]

The Pope, however, believed that with French assistance he could keep his temporal authority, and excuses were made as to why complete unification was impracticable. Odo Russell, nephew of Lord John Russell and unaccredited British agent at the Vatican from 1858 to 1870, reported that the Pope said to him in 1861: "'Do you know what Italian unity means? It means a nation of five and twenty millions harbouring more talent, mind and energy than any nation in the world, with an army of three hundred thousand men and a fleet of three hundred ships . . . Italy left to herself would soon be the first of the Great Powers of the world, and therefore the Five Powers of Europe will ever prevent her unity.'

"The first of the Great Powers"

'Your Holiness,' I replied, 'has now spoken as you did at the commencement of you reign, and then all Italy was at your feet, you were the national idol. But since Your Holiness has allowed foreign bayonets to stand between yourself and your people, they have turned to the only Italian power left to seek the realization of their wishes. But the day that Your Holiness will extend your hand to Piedmont and say, 'Let all hostilities cease, there shall be peace in Italy,' then the people will bless the name of Pius IX and the great work will be accomplished.'

'No, it will not,' the Pope again exclaimed, 'and you do not believe what you say!'

'And who is to prevent it,' I asked, 'if Your Holiness and Italy agree?'

In 1863, Pope Pius IX for the first time allowed the building of a railway into Rome. He is seen here standing in his special open saloon carriage

'The Great Powers of Europe,' the Pope replied.

'With the Pope's blessing and England's moral support, Italy has nothing to fear from them.' "[167]

It was true that the Papal territories around Rome relied for their defence on the guarantees of the great powers. Odo Russell, writing to Lord Russell on 2nd April 1861, stated that "The Vatican and the French authorities in Rome having made up their minds that the only solution of the Roman question is a permanent French occupation, the ex-King of Naples has also made up his mind to establish himself in Rome with his Queen . . . The priests talk a great deal about a proposed occupation of Romagna by the Austrians (which would be the product of a prolonged occupation of Rome by the French) and of the final *France and* execution of the Treaty of Villafranca, by the combined forces *Austria* of France and Austria . . . I am quite aware that the language of French officials is generally founded on nothing at all, but nevertheless I mention it to you that you may know what they think it necessary to talk about in the Eternal City . . . ."[167]

Writing again to Lord Russell in December 1861, Odo Russell described the various solutions to the Roman Question which had been debated. "Essentially these are but three: first, either the whole of the lost provinces of the Holy See are reconquered and held by foreign troops for the Pope as they were since 1849, or second, the total loss of the temporal dominions is acknowledged and the principle of a free church in a free state is adopted, or third, a portion only of the territory surrounding Rome is assigned to the Pope and must equally be held by foreign troops as is now the case . . . Of these three solutions the Pope will only admit the first, the Italian Government has proposed the second, and France is practically carrying out the third."[168]

The attitude of the Pope continued to harden, especially after *Garibaldi tries* an attempted march on Rome by Garibaldi in June 1862, which, *again* however, was foiled by the politicians before it was properly under way, though Garibaldi himself was shot in the foot. While Garibaldi returned to his farm to plot new moves, in 1864 a political attempt was made to solve the Roman question. By the September Convention, Napoleon III agreed to withdrew his troops from Rome within two years, and pledged himself to

The Austrian defeat of the Italians at Lissa, in the Adriatic, was the first full-scale battle between ironclad steamships

Franco-Italian Convention observe the principle of non-intervention. In return, Italy would guarantee the Pope's territory against attack, and would transfer its capital from Turin to Florence. The French minister, M. Drouyn de Lhuys, declared: "Of course in the end you will go to Rome. But it is important that between our evacuation and your going there, such an interval of time and such a series of events should elapse as to prevent people from establishing any connection between the two facts. France must not have any responsibility."[169]

Now that the absorption of Rome began to seem inevitable, primary objective of Italian leaders became the acquisition of Venice. In January 1866 Italy even offered to purchase it from Austria for 1,000 million lire, but this was rejected. Later in the same year, however, war broke out between Austria and Prussia, who were competing for domination over the smaller German states, and Italy saw a chance of winning Venice by allying with Prussia.

Austro-Prussian War The Prussians fought brilliantly, and won the great victory of Sadowa on 3rd July, which decided the war. Their Italian allies, however, were defeated on land at Custozza on 24th June, and at sea at Lissa on 20th July. In both battles the superiority in numbers of the Italians was rendered useless by incompetence in the higher command.

106

The people of Venice celebrate their liberation from Austria with a carnival and masquerade

Only Garibaldi and his volunteers in the Alps had any success, but jealousy of him had already caused divisions among the regular generals, and the government only allowed him inferior equipment. His personal power over his men, and the demands he made on their courage, enabled him to overcome this. One of his orders to his volunteers in the Trentino read: "Officers should be assiduous in the moral instruction of their men, personally conducting the discussions in camp and explaining the reasons for each victory or defeat. They must explain that brave people are always victorious and suffer few casualties, whereas those who flee from the enemy are much more easily picked off."[171]

Despite the defeats, Italy undoubtedly helped Prussia to win the war since Austrian troops had to be kept on the Italian front. As payment, Venice was at last ceded to Italy. Victor Emmanuel declared: "This is the most beautiful day of my life . . . The Austrians have restored to me the Iron Circlet of Italy, but far above it I place, what is dearest to me, the crown of my people's love."[172] The Venetians did not forget the patriot who had once inspired them to fight for freedom. In 1868 the body of Daniele Manin was brought home to Venice to rest in the Cathedral of St. Mark.

Venice liberated

107

Overleaf The Garibaldians (in the distance) are attacked by French and Papal troops at the battle of Mentana

The peace settlement required that Italy should give the Trentino back to Austria. Garibaldi was reluctant to abandon his occupation, since the area was inhabited mainly by Italians. He only retired when he received an explicit order from Victor Emmanuel, which he answered with a brief telegram: "I obey."

Congress for Peace

Garibaldi was the chief guest at an International Congress for Peace held at Geneva in 1867. He apologized that his proposals might not all be relevant, but hoped his audience would bear with him because of the strength of his feelings. He said:

"1. All nations should be regarded as sisters.

2. War between them should be thought of as impossible.

3. All international quarrels ought to be decided by a Congress.

4. The members of this Congress should be democratically elected.

5. All peoples, however small, should have the right of representation at this Congress.

8. The priesthood of revelation and of ignorance should be replaced by one of wisdom and intelligence.

9. Democracy alone can put an end to wars.

10. The only legitimate wars are those where a tyrant is opposed by those he has enslaved."[173]

The French leave Rome

In accordance with the September Convention of 1864, the French garrison left Rome in December 1866. Antonio Gallenga, a writer and revolutionary who had taken part in a plot to assassinate Charles Albert in 1833, gives a description of the Pope at this time: "Although he was at heart pious and forgiving, he would all at once be mastered by fits of ill-humour and spite, and often terminate with bitter irony and withering scorn a speech remarkable at the opening for its tone of Christian charity and resignation."[174] An example of this is the speech addressed to the French officers leaving Rome in 1866. The Pope was bitter at his desertion by Napoleon III, now himself very sick. "Go, my sons, with my blessing and my love. If you see the Emperor, tell him that I pray every day for him. I am told he is ailing, and I pray for his body . . . But if I pray for him he must do something for me, because he bears the title of the Most Christian, and France is the eldest daughter of the Church."[175]

The French withdrawal meant that no foreign troops remained in Italy, but the government could not take advantage of this to incorporate Rome into the new state because of its promise to Napoleon III. Garibaldi, however, was impatient to put an end to Papal rule. After attending the Geneva Conference, he planned to collect a band of volunteers, enter the Papal States from the north and march on Rome, hoping to promote a revolt in the city. Victor Emmanuel and Urbano Ratazzi, the Prime Minister, took an ambiguous attitude towards the adventure. Certainly arms were given to Garibaldi with government connivance, and large numbers of volunteers were given a free train ride to the frontier. The support could not be open, however, and when the force ran into difficulties and Mazzini failed to persuade the Romans to revolt, the state could give no further help.

Napoleon sent back a French army, armed with the new chassepot rifle, to help the 11,000 Papal troops. The latter, the Zouaves, were fervent Catholics recruited from all over the world, particularly Spain and Ireland, and fought with a fanaticism which perhaps surpassed the patriotism of Garibaldi's force. The weary, ill-equipped redshirts were defeated by the French and Papal armies at Mentana on 3rd November 1867.

The French return

The whole episode was a disaster. Garibaldi escaped across the border, only to be arrested by the Italian government. After three weeks he was sent to his home on the Isle of Caprera, where his movements were closely watched. By their refusal to revolt, and by welcoming the French as liberators, the Romans had cast into doubt the popular success of the whole struggle for unification.

The Romans oppose unity

The killing of six hundred Italian volunteers, however, caused such a shock in the country that the end of the Pope's temporal power became inevitable. However at the time it was easy to stir up extreme Catholic hatred against Garibaldi. These are the views of a Jesuit published in *La Civilta Cattolica* of Rome in 1867–8: "The valour of our small army will go down in history and is only to be explained by supernatural intervention . . . Such was their abnegation that often they had to march or fight for whole days without food and in heavy rain. Many had no bed to sleep in for three weeks on end, and had to be content with snatching an occasional nap in a haystack or on the bare ground. Their piety was exemplary. Officers and soliders confessed and went to mass before fighting; and then, having made peace with God and been given celestial grace, they threw themselves like lions into the battle."[176] The writer was only prepared to credit Garibaldi with "the kind of courage and success that befit a bandit leader from the woods," and regarded him as little more than a puppet. "We in Italy all know these dolls made of painted rags and sticks. The puppeteer can dress them as king or clown alternately . . . he can make their voice angry or insinuating, bitter or lively, happy or discontented; he can bring them on to the stage as he wishes, and then hang them up in his locker until the time comes to pack up and move to a new place."[177] Few people except his immediate enemies would accept that there was any truth in this portrait of Garibaldi; he had been prepared to disobey orders from wherever they came, and had fought for what he believed to be right even when for a long time his cause had seemed hopeless.

On 8th December 1869, the First Vatican Council, a meeting of all the bishops and cardinals, of the Catholic Church, as-sembled. On 20th July 1870 it issued its most significant state-ment, and one which was hardly calculated to make the Church more popular: the doctrine of Papal infallibility. "When the Roman Pontiff, in the fulfilment of his mission as the first teacher of all Christians, defines that which ought to be observed in matters of faith and morals, he cannot err."[178]

*"The Pope . . .
cannot err"*

The Pope's secular power in Rome was, however, already coming to an end. On 2nd August 1870, because of the Franco–Prussian War, the Rome garrison was recalled to France. The terms of the September Convention were brought into force for the second time. However, one phrase in the Convention gave Italy the loophole she needed: "In the case of extraordinary events, both the contracting parties would resume their freedom of action." Four days later an "extraordinary event" materialized – the crushing defeat of Napoleon III's army, and its surrender to the Prussians at Sedan in Lorraine.

*Prussia
defeats France*

A last-minute appeal to avoid bloodshed was made by Victor Emmanuel. He sent an envoy who said to the Pope, "Most Holy

Italian troops enter Rome through the breach in the walls, to complete the unification of Italy

Father, I address myself, as before, to Your Holiness' heart, with the affection of a son, the faith of a Catholic, the spirit of an Italian . . ."[179] The last sixteen words were but a poor plagiarism of King Charles Albert's when he introduced his constitution in 1847, and must have sounded like mockery to the Pope. Victor Emmanuel gave as his reason for wanting the Italian army to enter Rome the need to keep order throughout the Peninsula owing to the Franco-Prussian War. The Pope was angry, since with 13,000 of his own troops he was in no danger in Rome. He told the envoy that his masters were "white sepulchres and vipers," and that neither he nor his friends would enter Rome. Pius in fact realized that the end of his temporal rule was near, and called back the retreating envoy and said with a smile, "but that assurance is not infallible!"[180] In fact he had made it clear that he would yield only to violence and reserved the right to make at least a formal resistance to the Italian army.

Italy demands Rome

113

On 12th September, General Raffaele Cadorna's troops crossed the frontier and by the 20th were at the gates of Rome. Until the last moment the Italian government hoped for a popular rising in the city as an excuse for entry, but the Roman people did nothing.

The Pope is quoted by some writers as having addressed the following letter to the commander of his forces, General Kanzler: ". . . the defence should only consist in such a protest as would testify to the violence done to us, and nothing more; in other words, that negotiation for surrender should be opened as soon as a breach should be made."[181] In fact the fighting lasted for five hours, and, according to A. Gallenga, "The Pope seemed to expect that the avenging angel might at any time appear, smite the enemies, and then turn upon him, God's Vicar

Pius IX gives up as he was, and reproach him for his impatience and little faith."[182]

At last, after some nineteen Papal soldiers and forty-nine Italians had been killed and Cadorna had made a breach in the walls at Porta Pia, the Pope ordered the surrender.

Although the Italians had hoped for a popular uprising, Garibaldi and Mazzini had been kept under supervision to make sure that they did not intervene. Now it was essential to prove that the Romans had wanted unification. Plebiscites were held in the conquered territory, and an overwhelming majority (133,681 as against 1,507) voted in favour of annexation. The defeated side's view of this procedure is given by the Count of Beaufort, one of the Papal Zouaves, writing of the day before the plebiscite in Rome. "The walls were plastered with notices proclaiming in gigantic letters: *Yes We Want Annexation*. Through-

A rigged election? out the whole day of 1st October, voting cards were distributed marked with the annexationist *Yes*; and in the Corso a French engineer attached to the Acqua Maria works was arrested and detained for an hour at the police station for having dared to ask out loud for a card marked *No*."[183] No close check was kept on the system of voting. "To deposit a voting paper one had to show an elector's card; but besides the fact that this card was given indiscriminantly to all who asked for it, even to foreigners, it was not withdrawn when voting had taken place . . ."[184]

114 This meant that a number of enthusiasts were able to deposit

unlawful *Yes* votes in the ballot boxes of as many places as their legs could carry them.

In July 1871, Rome became the official capital of Italy. The Law of Guarantees, passed in 1870, applied Cavour's principle of a "free church in a free state." It allowed the Pope full sovereignty within the Vatican City, the part of Rome containing St. Peter's Cathedral and the main church buildings. He was also offered an annual payment of more than three million lire as compensation for the loss of his temporal sovereignty in the former Papal territories. The Pope however refused this and stubbornly refused to accept his new status, exhorting all Italian Catholics not to take part in politics as deputies or even *Catholic* as voters. Pius IX died in 1878, but his attitude towards the new *opposition* Italy was maintained by his successors. For the politicians, it was not urgent to find a solution to the "Roman Question" now that its power in the city had been secured. For many Italian Catholics, however, it meant that they could never give undivided loyalty to the new state. Thus the position of the government was still a precarious one.

Italy still faced serious economic and political problems. New industries were encouraged, but it was the already-prosperous northern cities which gained most from these. Weak leadership and the existence of many different political parties led to an unstable system of government, which was constantly depen- *Administrative* dent on coalitions and unable to pursue any continuous policy. *instability* People in the south complained increasingly that the government showed no concern with their problems of poverty and backwardness, but in reality these were geographical rather than political problems. And although democracy had been one of the aims of many leaders of the Risorgimento, it was not until 1912 that all men over thirty were given the vote.

Italy tried to establish her importance by joining in the manoeuvring of the Great Powers, and in 1882 joined the Triple Alliance with Germany and Austria. When the First World War eventually took place, however, and there seemed to be an opportunity to gain territory from Austria, Italy joined in on the side of Britain, France and Russia. She gained the Southern Tyrol and Venezia Giulia, areas with Italian-speaking majorites.

Austria was soon reconciled with Italy – here Victor Emmanuel is shown
visiting a horse show in Vienna in 1873

Many Italians were dissatisfied with the peace terms and with
the government's handling of the post-war economic problems.
In 1922, after his famous March on Rome, Mussolini came to
power as a dictator. He hoped that through his nationalistic,
Mussolini anti-democratic system of Fascism, he would lead the Italian
people to glory abroad and would give the country a prosperous
modern economy. His only real achievement, however, was
to solve the "Roman Question." By the Lateran Treaties of 1929,
Pope Pius X agreed to recognize the new Italian state.

Meanwhile Mussolini caused international crises by his
attempt to conquer Abyssinia in 1936, and by sending troops
to help the nationalists in the Spanish Civil War. Eventually he
116 led Italy into the Second World War in support of Hitler's

Germany, and was disastrously defeated. Since 1945, Italy, helped by her membership of the Common Market, has become more prosperous than ever before. The old problems of the division between north and south still remain, however, and many Italians still support the Communist and neo-Fascist parties which threaten to overthrow the present democratic government.

A. J. Whyte has summarized the various contributions to unity: "Every resource was called into action: poets and writers, politicians and orators . . . The one free kingdom, Piedmont, found soldiers and statesmen and the royal house for Italy . . . Conspirators and filibusters, inspired by Mazzini and Garibaldi, with utterly inadequate resources and by the most unprincipled methods, yet filled with the highest aims and the purest spirit of self-sacrifice . . . flung themselves into the struggle, defying governments and armies alike . . . France and England and Prussia had all to make their contribution. Exiles carried the cry of liberty and independence across the world, irritating governments, causing trouble everywhere, but never ceasing to protest and conspire."[185]

"Purest spirit of self-sacrifice"

Table of Dates

1821   Revolts in Naples and Piedmont put down by
        Austrian troops.

1830   Rebellion in the Papal States. Intervention of the
        French and Austrians.

1831   Failure of uprisings in Modena, Parma and the
        Papal States.

1833   Failure of Mazzini's plot against Piedmont.

1834   Failure of Mazzini's plot to invade Savoy.

1843   Failure of Mazzini-inspired plans for a
        co-ordinated rebellion in Naples, the Papal
        States and Tuscany.

        Publication of Gioberti's *Primato*.

1844   Publication of Balbo's pamphlet *On the Hopes of
        Italy*.

        Failure of expedition to Calabria, led by the
        Bandiera brothers and inspired by Mazzini.

1846   Election of Bishop of Imola to be the new Pope,
        Pius IX.

        Amnesty granted by the Pope to all political
        prisoners.

        Publication of D'Azeglio's book *Recent Events in
        Romagna*.

1847   Austrian troops occupy Ferrara in the Papal
        States.

        Modest liberal reforms introduced in Piedmont.

1848   Tobacco campaign and riots start in Milan.
        (1st January)

        Rebellion in Palermo, Sicily. Ferdinand II is
        forced to activate the 1812 constitution (12th
        January).

        Charles Albert grants a constitution to Piedmont
        (4th March).

Five day battle in which Milanese citizens managed to expel Austrian troops (18th March).

Austrian troops expelled from Venice, which proclaimed itself a republic (22nd March).

Sicily declares its independence from Naples (18th April).

Piedmont defeated by Austrian troops under Radetsky at Custozza (25th July).

Flight of Pope Pius IX from Rome to Naples (24th November).

1849   Rome is declared a republic (5th February).

Piedmont defeated by Austria at Novara. Charles Albert abdicates (23rd March).

Fall of the Roman Republic (30th June).

Sicily recovered by Ferdinand II. (May).

1852   Cavour becomes Prime Minister of Piedmont (4th November).

1855   Piedmontese troops take part in Crimean War (January).

1857   Formation of the *National Society*.

1858   Attempted assassination of Napoleon III by Felice Orsini (14th January).

Meeting between Napoleon III and Cavour at Plombières (20th July).

1859   Alliance between France and Piedmont against Austria (January).

Austria declares war on France and Piedmont (23rd April).

Battles of Magenta and Solferino (June).

Peace of Villafranca between Napoleon III and Franz Josef (11th July).

1860   Tuscany, Modena, Parma and Romagna join Piedmont in a new Italian state (January).

Revolt in Palermo (4th April).

Landing of Garibaldi's Thousand at Marsala, Sicily (11th May).

Battle of Milazzo. Garibaldi crosses the Straits of Messina (20th July).

King Francis leaves Naples for Gaeta. Garibaldi becomes Dictator of Naples (6th September).

Piedmontese troops defeat the Papal army at Castelfidardo (18th September).

Lord John Russell's Dispatch to the European powers (October).

Battle of Volturno (1st October).

Plebescites in Naples and Sicily (21st October).

1861   Francis II retires to Rome (February).

Victor Emmanuel II, King of Piedmont is proclaimed King of Italy by the first Parliament in Turin (17th March).

Garibaldi hands over authority for southern Italy to Victor Emmanuel II (26th October).

1862   Garibaldi wounded at Aspromonte in Calabria after an attempted march on Rome.

1864   French–Italian convention over Rome.

1866   Allied to Prussia in the Austro-Prussian war, Italy is defeated on land at Custozza and on sea at Lissa (June–July).

March on Palermo (September).

French garrison leaves Rome (December).

1867   Garibaldi's attempted march on Rome checked by French and Papal forces. Battle of Mentana.

1870   French troops leave Rome (August).

France defeated by Prussia at Sedan (September).

Italian troops capture Rome (20th September).

Dramatis Personae

COUNT CAMILLO DI CAVOUR (1810–61)   Aristocrat, diplomat and architect of Italian unity. He gave up his commission as an engineering officer in 1832 when the authorities disliked his liberal views. In 1847 he founded the newspaper *Il Risorgimento*. Elected to the Piedmontese Parliament in 1848 he played an important role in planning the *statuo* (constitution). As Prime Minister in 1852 he helped modernize Piedmont so that this state could play a leading role in Italian unity. By sending a contingent to take part in the Crimean War he focused the attention of the powers on the Italian problem. He enlisted French aid against the Austrians in 1859 and a nucleus for a united Italy was formed when the northern states joined Piedmont in 1860. Through skillful diplomacy he prevented French intervention against Garibaldi's expedition to the South in 1860. He was a realist, and believed that only with a powerful foreign ally would Italy eventually gain freedom and independence.

GIUSEPPE GARIBALDI (1807–82)   Soldier, seaman and adventurer. He was born at Nice in Savoy. At the age of fifteen he ran away from home to become a seaman. He joined the "Young Italy" movement and later the Piedmontese navy. He raised a revolt in support of Mazzini's planned invasion of Savoy in 1833. After its failure he managed to escape. Condemned to death, he fled to South America where he took part in many local conflicts and learnt the art of guerilla warfare. In 1848 he fought in defence of the Roman Republic against the French and his famous corps of the "Hunters of the Alps" harrassed the Austrians in the

121

mountains in 1859. In 1860 he led the expedition of "The
Thousand," dressed in the famous red shirts, and managed to
conquer Sicily and Naples from the Bourbon King, Francis II.
He inspired great loyalty in his followers, many of whom thought
he could not be killed or wounded. In 1862 and 1867 he led two
unsuccessful attempts to capture Rome. Eventually he retired
and concentrated on farming on the island of Caprera, off the
coast of Sardinia.

Daniele Manin, leader of the revolution in Venice in 1848

DANIELE MANIN (1804–57)   Lawyer, scholar and revolutionary. He fiercely attacked the despotic methods of the Austrian government in Venetia. During the Ninth Scientific Conference in Venice in 1847 he took an active part. After demanding Home Rule for Venetia in January 1848 he was imprisoned. Later he was released and played a leading role in the defence of Venice during the rebellion of 1848–9. He was exiled when Venice surrendered, and went to France. He was a republican and believed in Venetian regional independence. Eventually he realised that only through giving support to the Piedmontese monarchy could Italian unity and freedom be achieved, and on his death-bed he signed the articles of the National Society. His son Giorgio was wounded fighting with Garibaldi at Calatafimi in 1860.

GIUSEPPE MAZZINI (1805–72) Prophet and idealist. He was born in Genoa and educated at the local university. In 1830 he joined the Carbonari and was banished in 1831 after taking part in a plot against the King. He formed the "Young Italy" league in Marseilles and was again exiled. In 1837 he moved to London. He tried to make his ideal of "Unity and Independence" appeal to a wider number of Italians. Believing in democracy, nationalism and republicanism he founded numerous societies, wrote many articles and gave many speeches to further his aims. He believed in the need for education and self-sacrifice and felt Italy could make itself free by its own efforts. He inspired many expeditions to Italy to keep alive the spirit of rebellion but these failed. He disapproved of the methods by which Piedmont eventually united Italy.

LOUIS NAPOLEON III (1808–73)   Nephew of Napoleon I, he became Emperor of France in 1852. In his youth he had been a member of the Carbonari and had taken part in the risings in Italy in 1830. He became Emperor after having been involved in the French Revolution of 1848. The failure of Orsini, an Italian patriot, to assassinate him in 1858 reminded Napoleon of his promise to Cavour to aid the cause of Italian unity. He sent an army to Italy which defeated the Austrians at Magenta and Solferino, but then made a separate peace with Emperor

123

Franz Josef. His problem was that his Catholic supporters opposed it since it would ultimately threaten the temporal power of the Pope in Rome and the Papal States. In return for his support of Cavour Napoleon obtained Nice and Savoy for France in 1860. He was deposed after the German invasion of France in 1870, and died in exile at Chislehurst in England.

VICTOR EMMANUEL II (1820–1878)   King of Sardinia (Piedmont), and first King of united Italy. He displayed great courage in command of a brigade at Novara in 1849, and succeeded to the throne on his father Charles Albert's abdication shortly afterwards. He reigned as a constitutional monarch, and was pleased that his people called him *Rè Galantuomo* (Honest King). He supported Cavour in his policy of uniting Italy with French help, and did much to ensure that the Italian people chose unity rather than separatist republicanism. He was proclaimed King of Italy in Turin in 1861, and nine years later made Rome his capital. His descendants reigned in Italy until a referendum in June 1946 made the country a republic.

Further Reading

The following is a list of some of the more useful books for a detailed study of Italian history during this period. The first three listed are particularly suitable for schoolchildren.

Ewarts Scudder, *Garibaldi,* Duckworth, London, 1934.
Denis Mack Smith, *Making of Italy 1796–1866,* Macmillan, London, 1968
Garibaldi and the Risorgimento, (Collected documents), Jackdaw, London, 1970

Alexandre Dumas, *On Board the Emma,* Ernest Benn, London, 1929
Christopher Hibbert, *Garibaldi and His Enemies,* Longmans Green, London, 1960
Edgar Holt, *Risorgimento – The Making of Italy*, Macmillan, London, 1970
Evelyn Martinengo-Cesaresco, *Italian Characters in the Epoch of Unification,* T. F. Unwin, London, 1890
Joseph Mazzini, *The Duties of Man,* J. M. Dent, London, 1907
John Parris, *The Lion of Caprera,* Arthur Barker, London, 1962
G. Salvemini, *Mazzini,* (trans. I M. Rawson) University Press, 1956
Denis Mack Smith, *Cavour and Garibaldi 1860,* Cambridge University Press, 1954
George Macaulay Trevelyan, *Garibaldi's Defence of the Roman Republic, Garibaldi and the Thousand,* and *Garibaldi and the Making of Italy*, all Longmans, Green, London, 1911
A. J. Whyte, *Evolution of Modern Italy,* Basil Blackwell, Oxford, 1934

Notes on Sources

1 Woolf, *The Italian Risorgimento* Documentary extracts (London, 1969)
2 Mazzini, *Italy, Austria and the Papacy* (London, 1845)
3 Quoted in Mack Smith, *Italy: A Modern History* (Ann Arbor, 1959)
4 Woolf, *op. cit.*
5 Martin, *The Red Shirt and the Cross of Savoy* (London, 1969)
6 Woolf, *op. cit.*
7 Flagg, *Venice, the City of the Sea* (New York, 1853)
8 Trevelyan, *Manin and the Venetian Revolution of 1848* (London, 1923)
9 Pellico, *My Prisons* (London, 1963)
10 *Ibid.*
11 Woolf, *op. cit.*
12 Mazzini, *Life and Writings of Joseph Mazzini*, Vol. I (London, 1869)
13 *Ibid.*
14 *Ibid.*
15 Bayley, *Making of Modern Italy* (London, 1919)
16 Mazzini, *The Duties of Man* (London, 1907)
17 Mazzini, *Life and Writings of Joseph Mazzini*, Vol. I *op. cit.*
18 *Ibid.*
19 *Ibid.*
20 Mazzini, *The Duties of Man, op. cit.*
21 *Ibid.*
22 Martinengo-Cesaresco, *Liberation of Italy* (London, 1895)
23 *Ibid.*
24 Mazzini, *Italy, Austria and the Papacy, op. cit.*
25 *Ibid.*
26 D'Azeglio, *Recollections* (London, 1868) Trans. Count Maffei
27 King, *A History of Italian Unity* (London, 1899)
28 Tschudi, *Maria Sophia* (London, 1905) Trans. Ethel Hearn.
29 *Ibid.*
30 Campanella, *My Life and What I Have Learnt in It* (London, 1874)
31 Maffei, *Brigand Life in Italy,* Vol. 2. (London, 1865)
32 *Ibid.* Vol. 1
33 *Ibid.*
34 *Ibid.*
35 *Ibid.*
36 *Ibid.*
37 Mazzini, *Italy, Austria and the Papacy, op. cit.*
38 Berkeley, *The Irish Battalion in the Papal Army of 1860* (Dublin, 1929)
39 Godkin, *Life of Victor Emmanuel II*, 2 vols. (London, 1879)
40 King, *op. cit.*
41 *Ibid.*
42 Woolf, *op. cit.*
43 *Ibid.*
44 D'Azeglio, *op. cit.*
45 *Ibid.*
46 *Ibid.*
47 Quoted in Holt, *Risorgimento* (London, 1970)
48 Farini, *The Roman State from 1815 to 1850* Vol. I (London, 1851) Trans. W. E. Gladstone
49 Quoted in Berkeley, *op. cit.*
50 Quoted in Hales, *Pio Nono* (London, 1956)
51 Trevelyan, *op. cit.*
52 Berkeley, *op. cit.*
53 King, *op. cit.*
54 Trevelyan, *op. cit.*
55 Mack Smith, Ed. *The Making of Italy 1796–1870*, selected documents (New York, 1968)
56 Martin, *The Red Shirt and the Cross of Savoy, op. cit.*
57 Mack Smith, *op. cit.*
58 Woolf, *op. cit.*
59 Bayley, *op. cit.*
60 Mack Smith, *op. cit.*
61 Flagg, *op. cit.*
62 *Ibid.*
63 Whyte, *The Evolution of Modern Italy* (Oxford, 1944).
64 Mack Smith, *op. cit.*
65 Bayley, *op. cit.*
66 Trevelyan, *op. cit.*
67 *Ibid.*
68 *Ibid.*
69 Campanella, *op. cit.*
70 *Ibid.*
71 *Ibid.*
72 Flagg, *op. cit.*
73 Dandola, *The Italian Volunteers* (London, 1851)
74 Godkin, *op. cit.*
75 Bayley, *op. cit.*
76 Godkin, *op. cit.*
77 King, *op. cit.*
78 Dicey, *Cavour* (London, 1861)
79 Mazzini, *The Duties of Man, op. cit.*
80 *Ibid.*
81 Mack Walker, *Plombières: Secret Diplomacy and the Rebirth of Italy* A Documentary Collection (London, 1968)
82 *Ibid.*
83 Martinengo-Cesaresco, *Cavour* (London, 1896)
84 Mack Walker, *op. cit.*
85 Woolf, *op. cit.*
86 Mack Smith, *The Making of Italy, op. cit.*
87 Orsini, *Memoirs and Adventures of F. Orsini*

(London, 1857) Trans. G. Carbonel

88 Mack Walker, *op. cit.*
89 *Ibid.*
90 Mack Smith, *The Making of Italy, op. cit.*
91 Mack Walker, *op. cit.*
92 *Ibid.*
93 Arrivabene, *Italy under Victor Emmanuel,* Vol. I (London, 1862)
94 *Ibid.*
95 *Ibid.*
96 *Ibid.*
97 *Ibid.*
98 Garibaldi, *Memoirs of Garibaldi* (London, 1931)
99 *Ibid.*
100 Mack Smith, *The Making of Italy, op. cit.*
101 Garibaldi, *op. cit.*
102 Arrivabene, *Italy Under Victor Emmanuel, op. cit.*
103 Martinengo-Casaresco, *op. cit.*
104 *Ibid.*
105 Arrivabene, *Italy under Victor Emmanual,* Vol 2, *op. cit.*
106 Bayley, *op. cit.*
107 *Ibid.*
108 Dumas, *On Board the Emma* (London, 1929) Trans. R. S. Garnett
109 *Ibid.*
110 *Ibid.*
111 Mack Walker, *op. cit.*
112 Martinengo-Casaresco, *Liberation of Italy, op. cit.*
113 *Ibid.*
114 Forbes, *Campaign of Garibaldi in the Two Sicilies.* (Edinburgh, 1861)
115 Arrivabene, *Italy under Victor Emmanuel* Vol. 2, *op. cit.*
116 Crispi, *The Thousand* Trans. Mary Prichard Agnetti.

117 Martinengo-Cesaresco, *Italian Characters in the Epoch of Unification* (London, 1890)
118 Bayley, *op. cit.*
119 Mack Smith, Ed. *Garibaldi* (New Jersey, 1969)
120 *Ibid.*
121 Abba, *The Diary of One of Garibaldi's Thousand* (London, 1962) Trans. E. R. Vincent.
122 Lampedusa, *The Leopard* (London, 1960)
123 Martinengo-Cesaresco, *Italian Characters in the Epoch of Unification, op. cit.*
124 Mack Smith, Ed. *Garibaldi, op. cit.*
125 Garibaldi, *Life of Garibaldi* (London, 1864)
126 Whyte, *op. cit.*
127 Crispi, *op. cit.*
128 *Ibid.*
129 Martinengo-Cesaresco, *The Liberation of Italy, op. cit.*
130 *Ibid.*
131 *Ibid.*
132 Scudder, *Garibaldi* (London, 1934)
133 Maffei, *op. cit.*
134 Forbes, *op. cit.*
135 Trevelyan, *Garibaldi and the Making of Italy* (London, 1933)
136 *Ibid.*
137 *Ibid.*
138 Tschudi, *op. cit.*
139 *Ibid.*
140 Trevelyan, *Garibaldi and the Making of Italy, op. cit.*
141 Arrivabene, *Italy under Victor Emmanuel,* Vol. 2, *op. cit.*
142 Tschudi, *op. cit.*
143 *Ibid.*
144 Mack Smith, Ed. *Garibaldi, op. cit.*
145 Mack Smith, *The Making of Italy, op. cit.*

146 Lampedusa, *op. cit.*
147 Forbes, *op. cit.*
148 Mack Smith, *The Making of Italy, op. cit.*
149 Mack Smith, *Italy: A Modern History, op. cit.*
150 Crispi, *op. cit.*
151 Maffei, *op. cit.*
152 Mack Smith, *The Making of Italy, op. cit.*
153 *Ibid.*
154 *Ibid.*
155 Tschudi, *op. cit.*
156 Maffei, *op. cit.*
157 *Ibid.*
158 *Ibid.*
159 *Ibid.*
160 *Ibid.*
161 *Ibid.*
162 Mack Smith, *Italy: A Modern History, op. cit.*
163 Mack Smith, *The Making of Italy, op. cit.*
164 *Ibid.*
165 Woolfe, *op. cit.*
166 *Ibid.*
167 *Ibid.*
168 *Ibid.*
169 Godkin, *op. cit.* Vol 2
170 Mack Smith, *The Making of Italy, op. cit.*
171 Mack Smith, Ed. *Garibaldi, op. cit.*
172 Bayley, *op. cit.*
173 Mack Smith, Ed. *Garibaldi, op. cit.*
174 Gallenga, *The Pope and the King* (London, 1879)
175 *Ibid.*
176 Mack Smith, Ed. *Garibaldi, op. cit.*
177 *Ibid.*
178 Bernard, *Italy: A Historical Survey* (Newton Abbott, 1971)
179 Hales, *op. cit.*
180 *Ibid.*
181 Gallenga, *op. cit.*
182 *Ibid.*
183 Mack Smith, *The Making of Italy, op. cit.*
184 *Ibid.*
185 Whyte, *op. cit.*

Index

Picture Credits

The author and publishers wish to thank those who have given permission for copyright illustrations to appear on the following pages: Radio Times Hulton Picture Library, 21, 28, 54, 56, 59, 72, 92, 101, 104, 107, 113; Mary Evans Picture Library, jacket, 35, 37, 50, 106, 108–9, 122. Pictures appearing on the following pages are the property of the Wayland Picture Library: *frontispiece*, 8, 13, 17, 25, 31, 41, 44, 46 (*both*), 47, 49, 62, 64, 65, 66, 67, 69, 77, 79, 80, 82, 83, 84, 85, 87, 90, 91, 93, 94, 98, 116.